Writing the Critical Essay

Eating
Disorders

An OPPOSING **VIEWPOINTS**® Guide

Lauri S. Friedman, *Book Editor*

Christine Nasso, *Publisher*
Elizabeth Des Chenes, *Managing Editor*

OPPOSING
VIEWPOINTS®
SERIES

GREENHAVEN PRESS
An imprint of Thomson Gale, a part of The Thomson Corporation

THOMSON
✦
GALE

Detroit • New York • San Francisco • New Haven, Conn. • Waterville, Maine • London

LIBRARY OF CONGRESS CATALOGING-IN-PUBLICATION DATA

Eating disorders / Lauri S. Friedman, book editor.
   p. cm. — (Writing the critical essay)
  Includes bibliographical references and index.
  ISBN-13: 978-0-7377-3641-0 (hardcover)
  ISBN-10: 0-7377-3641-0 (hardcover)
  1. Eating disorders—Juvenile literature.   I. Friedman, Lauri S.
  RC552.E18E2821132 2007
  616.85'26—dc22
                                        2006032706

Printed in the United States of America

CONTENTS

Examining the state of writing and how it is taught in the United States was the official purpose of the National Commission on Writing in America's Schools and Colleges. The commission, made up of teachers, school administrators, business leaders, and college and university presidents, released its first report in 2003. "Despite the best efforts of many educators," commissioners argued, "writing has not received the full attention it deserves." Among the findings of the commission was that most fourth-grade students spent less than three hours a week writing, that three-quarters of high school seniors never receive a writing assignment in their history or social studies classes, and that more than 50 percent of first-year students in college have problems writing error-free papers. The commission called for a "cultural sea change" that would increase the emphasis on writing for both elementary and secondary schools. These conclusions have made some educators realize that writing must be emphasized in the curriculum. As colleges are demanding an ever-higher level of writing proficiency from incoming students, schools must respond by making students more competent writers. In response to these concerns, the SAT, an influential standardized test used for college admissions, required an essay for the first time in 2005.

Books in the Writing the Critical Essay: An Opposing Viewpoints Guide series use the patented Opposing Viewpoints format to help students learn to organize ideas and arguments and to write essays using common critical writing techniques. Each book in the series focuses on a particular type of essay writing—including expository, persuasive, descriptive, and narrative—that students learn while being taught both the five-paragraph essay as well as longer pieces of writing that have an opinionated focus. These guides include everything necessary to help students research, outline, draft, edit, and ultimately write successful essays across the curriculum, including essays for the SAT.

Using Opposing Viewpoints

This series is inspired by and builds upon Greenhaven Press's acclaimed Opposing Viewpoints series. As in the parent series, each book in the Writing the Critical Essay series focuses on a timely and controversial social issue that provides lots of opportunities for creating thought-provoking essays. The first section of each volume begins with a brief introductory essay that provides context for the opposing viewpoints that follow. These articles are chosen for their accessibility and clearly stated views. The thesis of each article is made explicit in the article's title and is accentuated by its pairing with an opposing or alternative view. These essays are both models of persuasive writing techniques and valuable research material that students can mine to write their own informed essays. Guided reading and discussion questions help lead students to key ideas and writing techniques presented in the selections.

The second section of each book begins with a preface discussing the format of the essays and examining characteristics of the featured essay type. Model five-paragraph and longer essays then demonstrate that essay type. The essays are annotated so that key writing elements and techniques are pointed out to the student. Sequential, step-by-step exercises help students construct and refine thesis statements; organize material into outlines; analyze and try out writing techniques; write transitions, introductions, and conclusions; and incorporate quotations and other researched material. Ultimately, students construct their own compositions using the designated essay type.

The third section of each volume provides additional research material and writing prompts to help the student. Additional facts about the topic of the book serve as a convenient source of supporting material for essays. Other features help students go beyond the book for their research. Like other Greenhaven Press books, each book in the Writing the Critical Essay series includes bibliographic listings of relevant periodical articles, books, Web sites, and organizations to contact.

Writing the Critical Essay: An Opposing Viewpoints Guide will help students master essay techniques that can be used in any discipline.

Background to Controversy: The Color of Eating Disorders

In the last few decades, anorexia, bulimia, and other eating disorders have gained recognition as serious diseases. Though once considered to be a vain response to an irrational desire to be thin, eating disorders are now widely understood to be an attempt to impose control and order on a sufferer's life. But while gains have been made in understanding what causes eating disorders, work remains in widening the definition of who suffers from them. Eating disorders have long been considered to affect middle-class, well-educated white women. However, increasing evidence has shown that eating disorders affect women of all ethnic groups and income brackets.

One reason eating disorders in women of color have gone unnoticed is that for many years, white women with such problems were the only ones targeted for study by professionals. Experts conducted much early research on eating disorders on college campuses or in hospital clinics, where the majority of the patient population was white. Marian Fitzgibbon and Melinda Stolley, psychiatrists who specialize in eating disorder therapy, explain further. "For reasons related to economics, access to care, and cultural attitudes toward psychological treatment, middle-class white females were the ones seeking treatment and thus the ones who became the subjects of research."[1] But Fitzgibbon and Stolley report that today, nearly 8 percent of the women seen in their clinic are African American, and that African American women are more likely than white women to fast and abuse laxatives and diuretics to avoid weight gain.

Minority women who develop eating disorders tend to be young, well educated, and perfectionists—much like

7

Binge eating, anorexia, and bulimia have long been regarded as disorders that affect white, middle-class women.

their white counterparts. Researchers such as Becky W. Thompson, author of the groundbreaking book *A Hunger So Wide and Deep*, suggest that women of color have long struggled with eating disorders as a response to dealing with racism, sexism, poverty, and other abuses suffered by minority women. "Anorexia is no longer the 'Golden Girl Syndrome,' striking only affluent white women in the West," writes researcher Annamarie Ruelle. "Not only has it spread to other socioeconomic and ethnic groups in the US, . . . but also to Japan, which now has the highest rates of anorexia in Asia."[2]

Both eating disorder sufferers and their physicians are less likely to diagnose and treat eating disorders in minority women. One study conducted by Ruth Striegel-Moore, a psychology professor at Wesleyan University, found that while about 30 percent of white women (296 out of 985 studied) received treatment for their eating disorder, only one black woman out of 1,061 had received treatment. "Because eating disorders are so identified as being problems of white women, both the women with the disorder and the service providers may not think of these as problems of black women," explains Striegel-Moore. "The physician may not ask about it, and the woman herself may not think about it as an eating disorder or as a problem for which you go and seek help."[3] Being underdiagnosed for eating disorders hurts women of color in their attempt to recover from these life-threatening diseases.

Who suffers from eating disorders, what causes them, and how to treat them are each increasingly popular topics of study in the fields of nutrition, psychology, and sociology. To this end, *Writing the Critical Essay: An Opposing Viewpoints Guide: Eating Disorders* exposes readers to the basic arguments made about eating disorders

Researchers suggest that women of color are increasingly developing eating disorders in reaction to racism, sexism, and poverty.

"How soon can I start her on fad diets?"

and encourages them to develop their own opinions. Through skill-building exercises and thoughtful discussion questions, students will articulate their own thoughts about eating disorders and develop tools to craft their own essays on the subject.

Notes

1. Marian Fitzgibbon and Melinda Stolley, "Minority Women: The Untold Story," NOVA, December 12, 2000. www.pbs.org/wgbh/nova/thin/minorities.html.

2. Annamarie Ruelle, "Starving Consumers: Culture, Gender, and Consumerism in the Aetiology of Anorexia in Japan," Occasional Paper No. 30, Centre for Asia-Pacific Initiatives, December 2004. www.capi.uvic.ca/pubs/oc_papers/a-ruelle.pdf.

3. Quoted in Karen Lurie, "Anorexia and Race," ScienCentral News, July 23, 2003. www.science ntral.com/articles/view.php3?article_id=218392017.

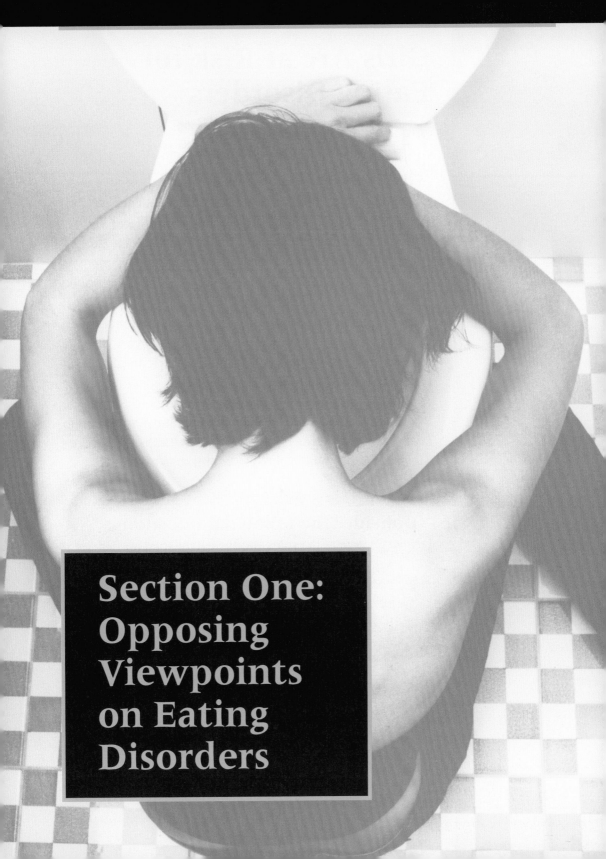

**Section One:
Opposing
Viewpoints
on Eating
Disorders**

Girls Are at Risk for Eating Disorders

Stephanie Booth

In the following essay, two girls recount their struggles with anorexia and bulimia. Brooke Casey and Denise Gray (not their real names) describe how each developed her eating disorder. Brooke became anorexic because she thought she could only feel good about herself if she was thin. Denise's bulimia began after her mother encouraged her to lose weight, saying that boys would not like her if she was fat. The girls then discuss their experiences with therapy and express their hopes for full recovery. Brooke and Denise are examples of many American girls who struggle with eating disorders.

Brooke and Denise related their stories to Stephanie Booth, a freelance writer whose stories have appeared in *Seventeen* magazine, *Teen Beat, Teen People,* and *Teen Magazine,* from which this viewpoint was taken.

Consider the following questions:
1. What were the rules Brooke established for herself regarding eating?
2. For what reason was Brooke hospitalized?
3. What effects did Denise's bulimia have on her body?

Before I became anorexic, people complimented me on how thin I was—not how pretty I was or how great I dressed. By high school, I thought being thin was my only positive physical attribute. It felt good knowing that I may

Stephanie Booth, "When Food Is the Enemy: Battling Against Eating Disorders," *Teen Magazine,* vol. 43, February 1999, p. 69. Copyright © 1999 by *Teen Magazine.* Reproduced by permission.

not be as cute as the cheerleaders, but I was skinnier. I started worrying that if I ever gained weight I'd become ugly.

Brooke Was an Anorexic

That's why I stopped eating all fast food and anything with
more than 2 grams of fat—basically, anything I liked. The
worse something tasted to me, the safer I felt eating it. I'd
usually have herbal tea for breakfast, a plain salad and
diet soda for lunch and a cup of white rice for dinner. I ate
slowly, trying to make every bite last. So many foods were
"bad" to me. The hot fudge sundaes and fried cheese I once
loved came to gross me out. When I felt hungry, I'd take a
bath or go to bed early. Drinking a lot of hot water filled
me up. I gave myself strict rules: no eating after 6 p.m., no

*Anorexics are often
obsessed with
exercising despite the
enormous toll it can
take on their bodies.*

eating more than half of anything and each time I walked into my kitchen—even for just a glass of water—I'd have to "pay" for it with 50 sit-ups.

I was in constant motion three hours a day to burn calories. I'd bike-ride, do exercise tapes or swim a mile at the YMCA (sometimes I'd walk the two miles there and back). Exhaustion made me forget how hungry I was.

In six months I went from 122 to 87 pounds—which felt more like 870 pounds to me. My jeans were hanging off of my 5-foot 6-inch frame, but I thought I looked huge. I was constantly freezing, even with long underwear and two pairs of wool socks on. Everyone would be wearing shorts while my fingers and toes would be turning blue.

My Life Became Endangered

My life was counting calories, weighing myself and standing nude in front of the mirror while I hunted for fat. I didn't have much energy. My grades dropped, and if it was a choice between exercise and going out with friends, I would sweat through two aerobics classes. Friends said, "You need to fatten up," but I thought they were jealous—I even thought my mom was. I'd get so mad when she asked, "Are you eating?" What was she trying to do—make me fat?

When I fainted in aerobics, everyone realized how bad I'd gotten. My body was so undernourished, I had to go to the hospital.

When I got there, the nurses asked me about my diet habits, and I totally lied. I know they must have been freaked out at the sight of me. My face was hollow and pointy, and my shoulder bones stuck out. The doctors took lots of blood and hooked me up to an IV to get some nutrients into my body. I stayed in the hospital overnight, and when I was released the next morning, the doctors gave me the name of an eating disorders specialist. Although I tried to deny the problem, it was obvious to them what was going on. They warned me that if I didn't change my habits, my life could be in danger.

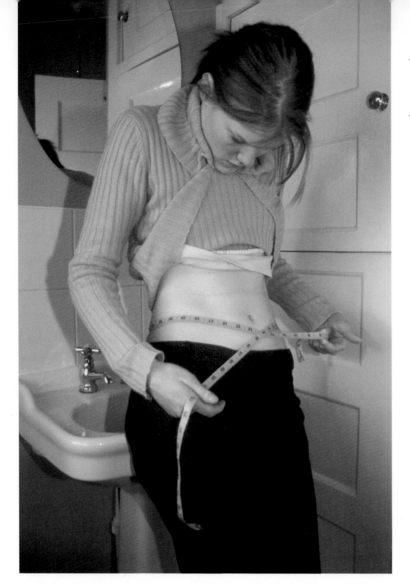

Although anorexics frequently weigh less than 100 pounds, they believe they are fat. This inability to accurately see themselves is part of the disorder.

The Road to Recovery

I'm sure going to a counselor saved my life. I promised my mom I'd go just once, without any intention of ever going back, but I liked Carol.

From the start, Carol explained that EDs [eating disorders] have a lot to do with how you feel about yourself. When I feel fat, what I'm really feeling is failure. I learned I was a total perfectionist. It was pathetic realizing how much I hated myself—I went through half a box of tissues that first visit.

A counselor works with a young eating disorder patient. Therapy is often a necessary part of overcoming an eating disorder.

Carol made me keep a log of what I ate. She taught me not to see food as "good" or "bad." It was a struggle. Wherever I went, I worried I would lose control and eat everything in sight. I even wondered if just smelling food caused weight gain. For months I didn't go to the movies because I'd have to smell popcorn. It was a huge triumph when I ate my first chicken sandwich in a year. I could only eat a third of it, and I felt I had to walk around the block afterward, but Carol said it was a baby step.

It's been two years since I was in the hospital, and I see Carol once a week. I'm on antidepressants, and my weight's up to 104. I'm trying to like myself more, but it's tough. "You're so skinny, it makes me sick," this girl at the mall said. I felt like responding, "You're right. It makes me sick too."

Denise's Story: Bulimia and Bingeing

The first time I threw up, I was 8 years old. I'd just seen a talk show on TV where all these women confessed they purged to keep their weight down. They'd eat as much as they wanted, then stick their fingers down their throats. I remember thinking, "I could do that." I was chubby and always trying to be as thin as my mom. She wanted me to be thin too—she put me on any diet she read about in magazines. "Boys would like you more if you weren't so fat," she said once when I complained about eating nothing but grapefruit all day. I didn't even

www.caglecartoons.com/espanol

Simanca. Copyright © 2004. Reproduced by permission of Cagle Cartoons, Inc.

like boys yet. When I was 10, my mom gave up bothering me about my weight. But I guess I was already brainwashed.

Now, every time I eat something, even an apple, I feel guilty, like I've let my mom down. She doesn't have to say anything; a little voice inside me screams, "How can you eat so much, you fat pig! You're so gross!" That's when I puke everything up. My life revolves around food—what I eat and when I throw up. We have four bathrooms at home, so it's easy to hide. I'm 5 feet 5 inches and have weighed anywhere from 90 to 150 pounds, but my parents still haven't caught on. At first, I mostly threw up dinner, but then I discovered bingeing.

Alternative Treatment Methods

The Renfrew Center [an eating disorder treatment facility] uses such nontraditional approaches as art therapy and dance therapy, to help patients find a creative outlet for their emotions, and a healing garden, where patients take care of plants and learn to nurture themselves in the process. . . . "Giving these women new interests and rituals replaces the negative rituals they have built around food," says [Renfrow training director Adrienne] Ressler.

Citation: Celeste Perron, "When a Diet Turns Deadly," *Cosmopolitan*, October, 2004, p186.

A Dangerous Fix

Now, if I'm feeling really bad about myself, usually if I had a crappy day or a fight with my parents, I sneak food into my room. Food fills me up and makes me feel better, but only for a few minutes. Then the misery hits. I'll go through a sack of candy corn, a loaf of bread and a bag of chips, and I drink lots of soda—it makes it easier to throw up. Waking up in the middle of the night to binge is like waking up on Christmas morning. It's sick, but that's how excited I get.

After I binge, I feel woozy and lightheaded—almost like getting laughing gas at the dentist. I feel almost happy. Then this guilt rises up inside me, and I have to stick my finger down my throat. I start crying when I'm puking. I worry I won't be able to get all the food back out. I keep gagging until I get the dry heaves. A couple of times, I jammed my finger down my throat so hard I scratched myself and tasted blood. I've spent so many hours with my head in the toilet, it doesn't disgust me anymore.

Purging, the act of making oneself throw up, causes staining and scarring to fingernails and teeth.

I Wouldn't Wish It on Anyone

All day long I bite my nails, thinking about when I can be alone so I can binge. Weekends are the worst, since my parents are home more often.

I'm not stupid. I know about bulimia. I know that stomach acid has worn the enamel off my teeth and that

I'm putting stress on my heart. Being bulimic is like being a smoker: You know it's not good for you, but you can't stop. I know I should talk to my parents, but I'm worried they'll be more disappointed in me. I've found some help on the Internet. There are a lot of girls like me, and we pour our hearts out to each other. Some of them don't think they're sick—they even trade puking tips. That's so sad. I wouldn't wish what I do or how I feel on anyone.

Analyze the essay:

1. Unlike some of the other viewpoints in this chapter, this essay was written in the first person. How did this influence your opinion of the authors' story? Would it have been as effective if Brooke's and Denise's stories were told in the third person?

2. In your opinion, what are the most effective descriptive details in this essay? Cite examples from the text in your answer.

Boys Are at Risk for Eating Disorders

Anorexia Nervosa and Related Eating Disorders

In the following essay, published by Anorexia Nervosa and Related Eating Disorders (ANRED), the authors argue that boys and men are at risk for developing serious eating disorders. Despite the fact that eating disorders are frequently considered a female problem, ANRED contends that anorexia and bulimia in males has become more common in the last twenty years. Some causes include pressure to be thin for a sport or a job and societal pressure to be thin to look good. The authors conclude that male struggles with eating disorders should be more widely recognized and that males should have better access to treatment resources.

ANRED is a private organization that seeks to educate the public about eating disorders and how to recover from them.

Consider the following questions:

1. According to the essay, what is the ratio of female anorexics to male anorexics?
2. How do the authors explain why eating disorder counselors see more female patients than male patients?
3. Why do the authors think that men and boys may be reluctant to admit they have an eating disorder?

The stereotypical anorexic, bulimic, and binge eater is female. The stereotype is misleading.

"Males with Eating Disorders," www.anred.com, January 16, 2006. Anorexia Nervosa and Related Eating Disorders, Inc. © 2005. All rights reserved. Reproduced by permission.

Just like girls and women, boys and men get anorexia nervosa and bulimia nervosa. Many males describe themselves as compulsive eaters, and some may have binge eating disorder. There is no evidence to suggest that eating disorders in males are atypical or somehow different from the eating disorders experienced by females.

Male Victims on the Rise

The numbers seem to be increasing. Twenty years ago it was thought that for every 10–15 women with anorexia or bulimia, there was one man. Today researchers find that for every four females with anorexia, there is one male, and for every 8–11 females with bulimia, there is one male.

Binge eating disorder seems to occur almost equally in males and females, although males are not as likely to feel guilty or anxious after a binge as women are sure to do.

Clinics and counselors see many more females than males, but that may be because males are reluctant to confess having what has become known as a "women's problem." Also, health professionals do not expect to see eating disorders in males and may therefore underdiagnose them.

What Causes Eating Disorders in Males?

Risk factors for males include the following:

- They were fat or overweight as children.
- They have been dieting. Dieting is one of the most powerful eating disorder triggers for both males and females, and one study indicates that up to seventy percent of high school students diet at one time or another to improve their appearance.
- They participate in a sport that demands thinness. Runners and jockeys are at higher risk than football players and weight lifters. Wrestlers who try to shed pounds quickly before a match so they can compete in a lower weight category seem to be at special risk. Body builders are at risk if they deplete body fat and fluid reserves to achieve high definition.

The pressure to have a perfect body is increasing the occurrence of eating disorders in males.

- They have a job or profession that demands thinness. Male models, actors, and entertainers seem to be at higher risk than the general population.
- Some, but not all, males with eating disorders are members of the gay community where men are judged on their physical attractiveness in much the same way that women are judged in the heterosexual community.

Social Obsession with Thinness Affects Men Too

Living in a culture fixated on diets and physical appearance is also a risk factor. Male underwear models and

Male athletes such as jockeys can develop eating disorders under the pressure to stay light and trim.

men participating in reality show make-overs lead other males to compare themselves with these so-called ideal body types. So do ads for male skin and hair care products. Weight loss and workout programs, as well as cosmetic surgery procedures, whose goal is chiseled muscularity can lead to the same sort of body dissatisfaction that afflicts women who read fashion magazines and watch movies and TV shows featuring "perfect" people.

In May 2004, researchers at the University of Central Florida released a study saying men who watched TV commercials with muscular actors felt unhappy about their own physiques. This "culture of muscularity" can be linked to eating disorders and steroid abuse, the researchers said.

Much has been made of the effect the Barbie doll has on the body image of a young girl. Now we have the Wolverine action figure (and others) marketed to boys. If Wolverine were life size, his biceps would be 32 inches around. Advertisers are marketing to males the same way they have pitched goods to females, with apparently many of the same related problems. . . .

Male Eating Disorder Victims Also Need Help

Because eating disorders have been described as female problems, males are often exceedingly reluctant to admit that they are in trouble and need help. In addition, most

Because eating disorders are typically thought of as female disorders, males with eating disorders may find it difficult to get help or treatment.

treatment programs and support groups have been designed for females and are populated exclusively by females. Males report feeling uncomfortable and out of place in discussions of lost menstrual periods, women's socio-cultural issues, female-oriented advertising, and similar topics.

Nevertheless, like females, males almost always need professional help to recover. The research is clear that males who complete treatment given by competent professionals have good outcomes. Being male has no adverse effect on recovery once the person commits to an effective, well-run program.

The wisest first step is a two-part evaluation: one component done by a physician to identify any physical problems contributing to, or resulting from, the eating disorder; and a second part done by a mental health therapist to identify psychological issues underlying problematic food behaviors.

When the two parts of the evaluation are complete, treatment recommendations can be made that address the individual's specific circumstances. . . .

It is important to remember that eating disorders in males, as well as in females, can be treated, and people of both genders do recover. Almost always, however, professional help is required.

Analyze the essay:

1. In this essay the authors discuss why men feel alienated from many eating disorder treatment programs. What are a few of these reasons? Do you find them to be believable? Explain your answer.

2. Describe the ways in which the essay says men are affected by societal pressures to be thin and good-looking. Do you agree with the authors that there is a "culture of muscularity" that can be linked to eating disorders?

The Media Causes Eating Disorders

Jessica Johnston

In the following viewpoint author Jessica Johnston argues that TV, magazines, movies, and advertisers cause women to develop eating disorders. She points out that the media frequently features women who are well below the average healthy weight, causing normal women to feel like there is something wrong with them. She also argues that the weight loss, fashion, and media industries have a vested interest in making women think they are too fat. If they believe this, she writes, then they will continue to purchase products that supposedly help them lose weight. She concludes that these industries should not be allowed to profit from encouraging a serious disease in millions of women.

Jessica Johnston is a writer for the socialist magazine *Justice*, from which this viewpoint was taken.

Consider the following questions:

1. According to the article, how much less does the average model weigh than the average teenager?
2. According to the author, eating disorders are rare in some parts of the world. Where are these places, and how does she account for this?
3. In what way, according to Johnston, does the media make even models feel that their appearance is not good enough?

"There's nothing wrong with me the way I am. However, when I look in the mirror I see a FAT girl named Jennifer. Not ever good enough or right enough

Jessica Johnston, "Eating Disorders: Symptoms of a Sick Culture," *Justice*, November 2004–January 2005. Reproduced by permission.

or pretty enough." That's how one anorexia victim described herself.

The prevalence of eating disorders in the U.S. has reached epidemic proportions, now afflicting 10–15% of Americans. This is no accident, but is the result of a profit-driven culture that overemphasizes physical appearance and idealizes thinness, particularly among women.

The Scope of Eating Disorders

The most well-known eating disorder, anorexia nervosa, is the third most common chronic illness among young women. Anorexic women suffer from the perception that they are overweight, when they are in fact often dangerously thin.

About 1 of every 10 people afflicted by anorexia will die of starvation, cardiac arrest, or another medical complication of the disease, making its death rate among the highest for a psychiatric disease.

Other common eating disorders include bulimia nervosa, in which a person binges and then purges themselves (usually by self-induced vomiting), and binge eating, in which a person cannot control their desire to overeat. While some men experience eating disorders, over 90% of people with them are women.

Thinness: The Most Important Virtue?

Usually only one body type is presented in the media and advertisements—a very tall, thin, often white woman who generally meets the weight criteria for anorexia as 15% below normal.

Many anthropology and psychiatry studies have shown that eating disorders develop in cultures that emphasize thinness as a socially important value. It is no accident

Most models are at least 15 percent below a normal woman's body weight.

that while eating disorders are rapidly increasing in Western countries, they are practically unknown in Asia, Africa, and many Middle Eastern countries.

Along with thinness, another major cultural myth fostered by TV, magazines, and movies is that a woman's physical appearance is more important than her ideas or accomplishments. This has led most women (and girls) in the U.S. to be overly concerned about their appearance. One survey of sixth grade girls found that 70% first became concerned about their weight between ages 9 and 11 (Shisslak et al., 1998).

And not only are eating disorders common, but in the past 30 years the number of American women afflicted by eating disorders has doubled. "I think we're seeing eating disorders in younger and younger individuals . . . as young as five or six," states Dr. Ira Sacker, director of the Brookdale University Hospital eating disorders clinic and co-author of *Dying to Be Thin*. According to *Time* magazine, 80% of all children have been on a diet by the time they reach fourth grade.

This is not surprising considering that while a teenager in the 1960s saw models that looked more or less like her, nowadays a teenager sees models that weigh on average 20% less than her.

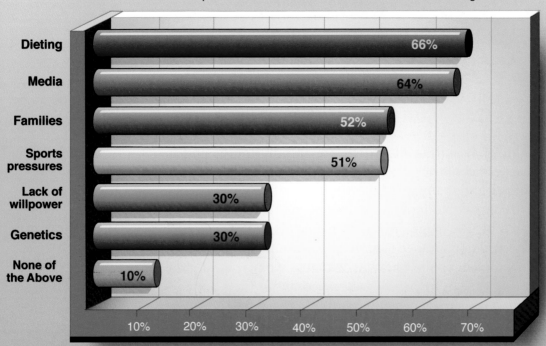

Causes of Eating Disorders: What Americans Believe

Results from a March 2005 poll reveal what factors Americans think cause eating disorders.

- Dieting: 66%
- Media: 64%
- Families: 52%
- Sports pressures: 51%
- Lack of willpower: 30%
- Genetics: 30%
- None of the Above: 10%

Source: National Eating Disorders Association (NEDA).

The Media's Standards Are Unattainable

Far from passively reflecting society, advertisements and the media create an entire cultural worldview, shaping people's attitudes and beliefs.

A good example of this is shown in a recent study conducted by Anne Becker in Fiji, where television was introduced as late as the mid-1990s. The study found that 83% of people felt TV had influenced their perceptions and thoughts about body image and size.

Advertising is particularly insidious because, in order to convince people to buy things, ads must make consumers feel that what they already have is not good enough. It requires making people feel the constant stress and anxiety of not being "attractive" or "fashionable" enough. Most of the time, even the "beautiful" models are not even considered good enough—photographs are airbrushed or otherwise altered to remove any lines, bumps, or "imperfections."

There is overwhelming evidence that the current body shape promoted by the fashion, cosmetics, and media industries is physically unattainable for 99% of women. This is no accident, because if the ideal of beauty is physically unattainable, then consumers will never be satisfied, and therefore there will be an endless demand for beauty products.

Making Girls Feel Guilty and Ashamed

As a result, the millions of women and girls who are unable to reach this standard of beauty feel a sense of failure, shame, and guilt. The Harvard Eating Disorders Center reports, in fact, that 80% of women wake up each morning feeling depressed about their appearance.

The success of this advertising is the reason for the incredible proliferation of the weight-loss, fashion, and beauty products industries, which are among the largest and most profitable consumer industries. But it is also a major cause of the incredible proliferation of eating disorders. . . .

Advertisements that feature impossibly thin women can make consumers feel inadequate and insecure.

The weight-loss, fashion, and media corporations are driven to bombard women with sexist messages that distort women's self-worth because of the nature of the capitalist system, which forces corporations to constantly expand their markets and sell more products in order to remain competitive and increase profits.

We Must Reject This Beauty-Obsessed Culture

To stop this sick logic of the profit system, we need to start by taking the weight-loss, fashion, and media corporations out of private hands and making them public property under democratic control and management. Only then could these industries begin to serve the public good rather than contributing to a growing epidemic of eating disorders.

Clearly, the hidden suffering of millions of women with eating disorders is not simply a personal problem, but a social one. Eating disorders are fundamentally caused by an alienating culture and psychology shaped by capitalism's insatiable lust for profits, which turns everything into a commodity to be bought and sold on the market. There can be no serious solution to the eating disorders epidemic without addressing its root cause by sweeping away the entire capitalist system and establishing a new socialist society based on human need, not corporate greed.

Analyze the essay:

1. The author suggests that advertisers need women to feel badly about their appearance so that they will continue to purchase beauty and diet products. What do you think of this idea—does it seem plausible? Explain your answer.

2. Johnston uses many statistics to back up her ideas. Go through her essay and list where she has used statistics to support her claims. How does her use of this information affect how you interpret her message?

Psychological and Biological Factors Cause Eating Disorders

Thom Hartmann

In the following essay Thom Hartmann argues that eating disorders are a symptom of psychological disorders that are genetically inherited. He explains that an obsessive fixation with one's appearance is a facet of obsessive-compulsive disorder (OCD), a mental illness in which a person feels extremely compelled to perform very narrow behavioral rituals. Obsessive-compulsive personalities may have neurotic physical habits or react irrationally to their possessions being out of order. Hartmann argues that victims of eating disorders exhibit OCD behavior when they irrationally focus on their weight or design complex rituals around food. While the media is not directly responsible for eating disorders, Hartmann explains that people who are genetically predisposed to being OCD tend to develop eating disorders when they see advertisements that make them feel inadequate or ugly.

Thom Hartmann is a former psychotherapist and the host of a nationally syndicated progressive talk show.

Consider the following questions:

1. According to Hartmann, what are SSRI drugs and what connection do they have to eating disorders?
2. What influence does upbringing have on whether a person develops an eating disorder, according to Hartmann?
3. Describe two health problems brought on by bulimia.

Years ago, a popular and wry sign to hang in one's office or on one's cubicle said, "A Clean Desk Is The Sign Of A Sick Mind." There is a very faint grain of truth to that, which highlights an opportunity for the media to use Terry Schiavo's[1] tragic situation to actually save lives of girls and women (and a few men) in non-vegetative states.

Many Attempts to Understand Eating Disorders

For years it was believed that anorexia (not eating) and bulimia (eating and vomiting or "purging") were signs of an exogenous "induced" (life-experience-caused) mental illness. The most common theories constituted a hodge-podge of ideas ranging from "bad parenting" and child abuse to the more Freudian "poor toilet training," and psychotherapy to treat anorexia and/or bulimia centered around trying to remember, bring out, relive, and/or relieve these "causes." These therapies rarely worked, and often made situations worse by focusing on the loci of the obsession.

Then along came the SSRI drugs—selective serotonin reuptake inhibitors—antidepressants like Prozac. In the course of researching these drugs, it was accidentally discovered that they were often successful in treating people with obsessive-compulsive disorders (OCD), and that people with anorexia and, particularly, bulimia responded well to them. (The downside of the SSRI's is that they cause lack of affect and increase the chances of suicide, as recent studies and the stories of so many school shooters on SSRI drugs show.)

Eating Disorders Caused By Genes, Psychological Disorders

This revolutionized psychiatry's perspective of these eating disorders, causing many in the field to conclude that

---

1. Terry Schiavo died in 2005 after being in a fifteen-year vegetative state brought on by her eating disorder.

they were really subsets of OCD, where the obsession had settled on body weight or image, instead of the traditional OCD flags such as hand-washing, magical thinking, or evening-up (counting syllables in road signs, touching with one hand what had been touched with the other, etc.).

It also implied that OCD was genetically mediated, had to do with variations in the levels of specific neurotransmitters (especially serotonin), had little to do with upbringing (other than experiences determining where the focus of the OCD would settle), and has been in the human genome for millions of years.

This last observation . . . has led some in the field to the conclusion that a certain level of OCD is useful and necessary for a functioning society, and that there's a touch—more or less—in all of us. It's what causes some people to keep their homes or garages super-neat, be fastidious about their appearance, or maintain that "clean desk" of office lore. In small doses, sub-clinical OCD works to keep us organized.

Obsessive-Compulsive Behavior to the Extreme

But slightly-above-average OCD levels also create a vulnerability in individuals who carry the genes for it, which the marketing industry recognized three decades ago when it began applying psychographic analysis to advertising strategies, and now aggressively exploits. Is your hair shiny enough? Are your teeth white enough? Is your body thin enough?

This genetic predisposition to sub-clinical (and thus "normal") OCD appears to make its carriers particularly vulnerable to advertising. As the BBC reported in 1999, just 38 months after the introduction of television to parts of Fiji, purging—bulimia—among teenage girls had gone from being virtually unknown to being something practiced by fully 15 percent of all young women. They "got it" that being "desirable" meant being thin, but didn't have the money to buy the weight aids advertised. The

A teenage girl pinches imaginary fat. Experts think an obsession with fat may stem from personality disorders such as obsessive-compulsive disorder.

cheaper solution was just to put a finger down the throat and upchuck the most recent meal.

Serious Health Risks for Victims

Bulimia can lead to a variety of problems. Gastro-intestinal reflux disorder (GIRD) is often the result of stomach acids burning the esophagus on their way up during purging,

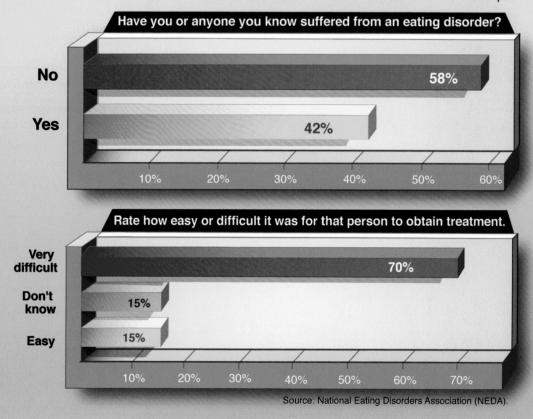

Eating Disorders Are Common

Four out of ten Americans either have or have had an eating disorder—or know someone who has. The information below is from a March 2005 poll.

Have you or anyone you know suffered from an eating disorder?

No — 58%
Yes — 42%

10% 20% 30% 40% 50% 60%

Rate how easy or difficult it was for that person to obtain treatment.

Very difficult — 70%
Don't know — 15%
Easy — 15%

10% 20% 30% 40% 50% 60% 70%

Source: National Eating Disorders Association (NEDA).

leading in some cases to a lifetime dependence on antacids or prescription stomach acid inhibitors. Teeth are eaten away by stomach acids. Nutritional deficiencies—particularly mineral deficiencies—abound. And in extreme cases the imbalance of minerals produced by this (particularly the lack of potassium) can cause heart attacks, such as the one that stopped the flow of blood and oxygen to Terry Schiavo's brain, leaving her in a persistent vegetative state.

As The National Association for Anorexia Nervosa and Associated Eating Disorders notes: "Anorexia has the highest mortality rate of all mental illnesses; a woman with anorexia is 12 times more likely to die than a woman her age without an eating disorder. Individuals with bulimia risk severe electrolyte imbalances, kidney disturbances, heart problems and other serious, life threatening medical complications."

Terry Schiavo gives us, at the end of her life, a gift—a chance to use her case to share with other young girls and women the outcome of anorexia and bulimia. In a larger and more important context, it provides us with an opportunity to open a culture-wide discussion of the psychological and—ultimately—physical dangers of exposure to personal-image-based advertising and marketing.

Analyze the essay:

1. This essay, which argues that eating disorders are caused by psychological disorders, is written by a former psychotherapist. How does the author's background influence your opinion of his argument?

2. Thom Hartmann and Jessica Johnston have different opinions on the extent to which advertising and the media cause eating disorders. Explain the ways in which their arguments differ. Whose argument do you agree with more?

How I Fell Victim to Pro–Eating Disorder Web Sites

L.A. Youth

In the following essay the author, an anonymous teenage girl, describes how she was sucked into the scary world of pro–eating disorder (called "pro-ana") Web sites. After stumbling upon Web sites that promote eating disorders as a desirable lifestyle, the author began starving herself and doing extreme exercise to lose weight. After realizing she was hurting herself, she critically examined the content of the Web sites and realized they glorified a serious sickness. She concludes that pro–eating disorder Web sites are a danger to young people who may be influenced by them.

This essay was featured in *L.A. Youth*, a newspaper produced by and for teens.

Consider the following questions:

1. According to the author, what ritual did she find described on pro–eating disorder Web sites?
2. Why do you think the author includes the anecdote about the girl who wanted to recover from anorexia?
3. According to the author, how should people defend themselves against pro-ana Web sites?

During vacation I practically lived online. As I surfed the Net and updated my online journal at Xanga.com late one night, I suddenly came across another random

"How Thin Do I Have to Be?" *L.A. Youth*, September 2005, pp. 10–11. Reproduced by permission.

girl's Xanga. It seemed normal enough, but then I noticed an inconspicuous link.

A World of Skin and Bones
Curious, I clicked on it and found cheerful pastel color schemes and attention-grabbing titles that seemed like an innocent teenage girl's Web site. I clicked on the "thinspiration" link and was sent to a picture of actress Calista Flockhart looking stunning in a red dress. As I

A photo of the very thin actress Calista Flockhart drew one young woman to a Web site promoting anorexia.

kept looking, the pictures gradually grew more graphic, showing women who were disgustingly thin. I was shocked because I didn't know that any human could ever look like these women did. They had no bodies; they literally looked like skin and bones.

While I glanced at the rest of the content on the site I found poetry about anorexia, nutritional information on "safe foods" and tips for keeping this habit a secret. I knew that anorexia was an eating disorder, but the Web site's slogan was, "Anorexia is a lifestyle, not a disease." I was so appalled by this Web site that I had to instant message my friend and tell her about it. The moment I told her she responded, "Oh my God, shut it down! Close it! Close it!"

I Couldn't Look Away

But I didn't. The pictures of the undernourished models and actresses sickened me, yet I couldn't look away. I shut down my computer and went to sleep but I dreamt about their skeletal appearances all night. The next day I went online and ended up back at the same Web site. There was something so alluring about these girls, smiling as they wasted away into nothingness.

As I became more intrigued, I started to read the poetry on the site. The poems were strangely touching, like one girl's "Self-destruction can be such a beautiful thing" while other poems were chillingly powerful, like "See the girl with the hollow eyes/ Hate the symptoms, love her size." These girls wanted love, attention and acceptance, just like everyone else. I related to their obsession with perfection; as much as they wanted to have the perfect body, I wanted to have the perfect grades. Just as they took pride with every five pounds lost, I savored every "A" I earned. These Web sites weren't about losing weight, they were about achieving

> ## Justifying a Disease
>
> People who support pro-eating disorder Web sites are wrongly justifying their disease and whether intentionally or not, are influencing people to join them.
>
> Gracie Doran, "Everything online should not be digested," Daily Evergreen, July 13, 2006. www.daily evergreen.com/story/18243.

perfection, and these girls weren't weirdos, they were girls like me struggling to be perfect, too, or so I thought.

The recent phenomenon of "pro-ana" Web sites has caused concern among parents, teachers, and teens alike.

Following the Tips

The more time I spent browsing these "pro-ana" Web sites, which promote anorexia, the more I began to criticize myself. I could see all of my own flaws: my flabby thighs, my chubby cheeks, everything was ugly. It's embarrassing to admit, but I started to follow the diet tips. I began to drink gallons of water and started to ban myself from foods that these sites labeled as "bad." I ate mint gum to make everything taste awful, and I even volunteered to wash the dishes so that my mom wouldn't notice that I hadn't eaten much of my dinner. Still, I saw no results, so I decided to try the exercise tips. Late one night, while everyone else was asleep, I looked at myself in the mirror and started to cry. How could I feel good about myself when everything online told me I was too fat?

One day I stayed up until two in the morning blasting Gwen Stefani's "Crash" from my stereo. For some reason, I couldn't sleep so I decided to try some of the exercises listed on some pro-ana sites in hopes of flattening my rebellious stomach. I did crunches and sit-ups until I lost count and began to feel dizzy. After I desperately tried to catch my breath, I decided I should stop exercising and go to sleep. The next morning, I was completely exhausted and there were weird dark red lines on my stomach. For the rest of that week I had trouble sitting down and it even hurt to laugh! At that moment I freaked out with the realization that I had been sucked into the world of anorexia without even knowing it.

Coming to My Senses

I was incredibly disappointed in myself. How could I be so stupid? . . . This experience made me aware of the dangers that these Web sites pose. I mean, I never thought that I would become influenced by a couple of pictures and some poems, but I'm not as strong as I thought. I'm human and I'm insecure, and after this experience I've realized that I'm also far from perfect.

When I started doing some real research, I found out that anorexia and bulimia involve more than merely a search for the perfect body. Eating disorders indicate severe emotional problems and people who suffer from anorexia avoid food for psychological reasons. Those who binge (eat large amounts of food in short periods of time) and later purge (make themselves vomit) are classified as bulimic. People who suffer from these eating disorders are often isolated from others so they can hide their disease. Maybe that's why many anorexic and bulimic people turn to the Internet to connect with others who have similar problems. . . .

No Interest in Recovery

But I found the Web site of another girl who vowed to recover from anorexia. She said she would no longer be updating her pro-ana site, which featured her artwork, poems, tips, tricks, links and much more. I was shocked to find that even though she had many online buddies, once she made the decision to recover, they turned on her. These supposed "friends" were now bombarding her with

Those struggling with eating disorders often fall into deep depression and may attempt to isolate themselves from friends and family.

Bone-thin models help perpetuate the idea that women should be skinny. Those with eating disorders are exceedingly vulnerable to such images.

triggering images—pictures of super-skinny men and women intended to encourage her to keep starving herself—and hate mail so that she had to shut down her e-mail account and cut off all contact from anyone online! . . .

A Sad and Confused World

As I continued to analyze the messages on these sites, they didn't seem to make any sense. One moment they claimed that it was healthy to set insane goals for their bodies through fasting, vomiting and excessive exercise, and the next they offered a step-by-step guide for a creepy ritual to summon some anorexic god! In this ritual, you offer tempting foods as sacrifices, say an invocation and then burn the foods. It's supposed to help you ward off food temptations and lose weight. . . .

The last time I visited a pro-ana site, I didn't feel any temptation to sneak a peek at the pictures because I was too angry and depressed to look at any of them. As I re-read the sections admiring bone-thin models, the encouraging essays on loving hunger, light-headedness, and nausea (all results from the fasts people subject themselves to) I started to feel incredibly sad. . . .

The Problem Is Widespread

There are literally millions of women and men suffering from eating disorders in the United States alone. An estimated 10 million females and one million males suffer from anorexia or bulimia, according to the National Eating Disorders Association.

Because of the many problems constantly going on around the world, people often forget about the struggles inside their own minds. There's the pressure to get good grades, to please our families, to be popular, to be beautiful, to be perfect—the list is never-ending. Sometimes we forget who we are and try to become who others want us to be. That's when pro-ana sites step in to take advantage of our insecurities. The only thing we can do to defend ourselves from these Web sites is to be happy with who we are, even if it's not always the easiest thing to do. I've learned my lesson not to define who I am by what size jeans I wear. There's more to me than that, and hopefully, other teens struggling with their self-images realize that too.

Analyze the essay:

1. What are the most compelling descriptive passages in this essay, in your opinion? How does the author enable the reader to visualize her experience with the pro-ana Web sites?
2. The author shares graphic examples of the pro–eating disorder Web sites' content in order to tell her story. How did these details enhance her story? Did you have enough information to picture what she had seen?

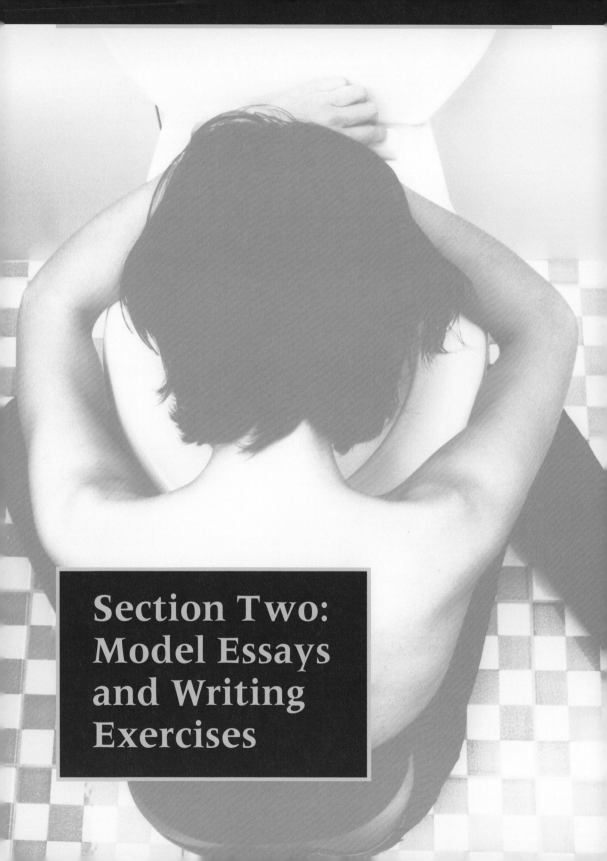

Section Two: Model Essays and Writing Exercises

The Five-Paragraph Essay

An essay is a short piece of writing that discusses or analyzes one topic. The five-paragraph essay is a form commonly used in school assignments and tests. Every five-paragraph essay begins with an introduction, ends with a conclusion, and features three supporting paragraphs in the middle.

The Thesis Statement. The introduction includes the essay's thesis statement. The thesis statement presents the argument or point the author is trying to make about the topic. The essays in this book all have different thesis statements because they are making different arguments about eating disorders.

The thesis statement should clearly tell the reader what the essay will be about. A focused thesis statement helps determine what will be in the essay; the subsequent paragraphs are spent developing and supporting its argument.

The Introduction. In addition to presenting the thesis statement, a well-written introductory paragraph captures the attention of the reader and explains why the topic being explored is important. It may provide the reader with background information on the subject matter or feature an anecdote that illustrates a point relevant to the topic. It could also present startling information that clarifies the point of the essay or put forth a contradictory position that the essay will refute. Further techniques for writing an introduction are found later in this section.

The Supporting Paragraphs. The introduction is then followed by three (or more) supporting paragraphs. These are the main body of the essay. Each paragraph presents and develops a subtopic that supports the essay's thesis statement. Each subtopic is then supported with its own facts, details, and examples. The writer can use various kinds of supporting material and details to back up the topic of each supporting paragraph. These may include statistics, quotations from people with special knowledge or expertise, historic facts, and anecdotes. A rule of writing is that specific and concrete examples are more convincing than vague, general, or unsupported assertions.

The Conclusion. The conclusion is the paragraph that closes the essay. Its function is to summarize or reiterate the main idea of the essay. It may recall an idea from the introduction or briefly examine the larger implications of the thesis. Because the conclusion is also the last chance a writer has to make an impression on the reader, it is important that it not simply repeat what has been presented elsewhere in the essay but close it in a clear, final, and memorable way.

Although the order of the essay's component paragraphs is important, they do not have to be written in that order. Some writers like to decide on a thesis and write the introduction paragraph first. Other writers like to focus first on the body of the essay and write the introduction and conclusion later.

Pitfalls to Avoid

When writing essays about controversial issues such as eating disorders, it is important to remember that disputes over the material are common precisely because there are many different perspectives. Remember to state your arguments in careful and measured terms. Evaluate your topic fairly—avoid overstating negative qualities of one perspective or understating positive qualities of another. Use examples, facts, and details to support any assertions you make.

The Descriptive Essay

The previous section of this book provided you with samples of published persuasive writing on eating disorders. Many of these essays used description to convey their message. In this section you will focus on developing your own descriptive writing skills.

A descriptive essay gives a reader a mental picture of the subject that the writer is exploring. Typically, descriptive writing uses the five senses—sight, sound, touch, taste, and smell—to help the reader experience what the writer has experienced. A descriptive writer carefully selects vivid examples and specific details to reveal people, places, processes, events, and ideas.

Using the Descriptive Essay

While an essay can be purely descriptive, descriptive papers written for the classroom are often persuasive or expository essays that use description to make a point. Writers may also rely on description as they explain a memory or discuss an experience. For example, in Viewpoint Five, an anonymous teenage girl describes how she was lured into the online world of eating disorders.

Sometimes, descriptive essays are written in the first person (from the "I" point of view). In these cases there is no one sentence that can be singled out as the thesis statement. Instead the essay has an implied thesis—a point of view made evident through the writer's careful use of details and examples.

Descriptive Writing Techniques

An important element of descriptive writing is the use of images and specific and concrete details. Specific and concrete is the opposite of general and abstract. Descriptive writers should give their readers a fuller understanding of the topic by focusing on tangible details and by appealing to the five senses. See the accompanying box for examples of general nouns and their more specific variations.

General	More Specific	Most Specific
vegetation	trees	fir
animal	fish	salmon
grocery item	breakfast food	cereal
sound	crash	broken glass
emotion	happiness	elation

The use of metaphors and similes can also enliven descriptive writing. A metaphor is a word or phrase that compares two objects that are dissimilar. A simile is a metaphor that includes the prepositions *like* or *as*. In Viewpoint Five the teenage girl published in *L.A. Youth* describes her experience with pro–eating disorder Web sites using a simile when she writes, "They had no bodies; they literally looked like skin and bones."

Some descriptive essays make use of scene and exposition. The scene is an element commonly found in fiction and in creative writing. With scene, a writer describes an event with moment-by-moment detail, often including dialogue if people are involved. With exposition, a writer explains, summarizes, or concisely recounts events that occur between scenes. Scene is comparable to showing, while exposition is similar to telling.

Tips to Remember

A descriptive essay should give the reader a clear impression of its subject. So, a writer must select the most relevant details. A few well-chosen details are more effective than dozens of random ones. You want the reader to visualize what you are describing but not feel overloaded with information. The room you are sitting in now, for example, is likely full of many concrete and specific items. To describe the room in writing, however, you would want to choose just a few of the most vivid details that would help convey your impression of and attitude about it.

A writer should also be aware of the kinds of words he or she uses in descriptive passages. Modifying words like adjectives and adverbs can enhance descriptive writing, but they should be used sparingly. Generally, verbs and nouns are more powerful than adjectives and adverbs. The overuse of modifying words makes the writing seem wordy and unnatural. Compare the phrases in the accompanying box to see the difference between wordy and concise language.

Wordy	Concise
bright green potted plant with thin leaves	fern
rolling around rapidly in brilliant, untamed magnificence	dancing in wild splendor
she stopped extremely abruptly	she stopped
the best most amazingly wonderful experience	a fantastic time

In the following section you will read some model descriptive essays about eating disorders and work on exercises that will assist you as you write your own.

Impossible Images: Advertising and Eating Disorders

Editor's Notes The first model essay examines the effect the media has on eating disorders. The author argues that advertisements set impossible standards for beauty that cause both men and women to develop self-esteem issues and eating disorders. The essay is structured as a five-paragraph essay that uses descriptive details and examples to develop the argument.

The notes in the margin point out key features of the essay and will help you understand how the essay is organized. Also note that all sources are cited using MLA style. For more information on how to cite your sources, see Appendix C.* While you read, consider the following:

- How does the introduction engage the reader's attention?
- What descriptive techniques are used in the essay?
- What purpose do the essay's quotes serve?
- Does the essay convince you of its point?

■ Refers to thesis and topic sentences

■ Refers to supporting details

Paragraph 1

Flip through the pages of any consumer magazine and you will see where the problem begins. Impossibly thin glamour girls strut around in revealing outfits that leave no room for imperfection. Bronzed, muscled, and shirtless men are the designated spokesmen for products such as razors, deodorants, even toothbrushes. The barrage of images American women and men see in advertisements sets an impossible standard for physicality. Unfortunately, these unrealistic standards of beauty can have dangerous consequences for people's mental and physical health.

This is the essays's thesis statement.

Paragraph 2

American women are pitched an impossibly thin standard by advertisers who hope to profit from their insecurity. Many

This is the topic sentence of Paragraph 2. Note how it encapsulates the main point of the pragraph.

* In applying MLA style, the following simplifications have been made: Parenthetical text citations are confined to direct quotations only; electronic source documentation in the Works Cited lists omits page ranges and some detailed facts of publication.

advertisements present outrageously skinny women—the minority of the population—as if they are the norm. Indeed, if earth's population were to be judged solely by the advertisements in magazines, it would appear that the entire female population was 5'11" and 117 pounds, which is certainly not the case. In fact, the average model weighs about 23 percent less than the average American woman, according to the Student Nutrition and Action Committee at the University of California, Los Angeles. Says writer Jessica Johnston, "There is overwhelming evidence that the current body shape promoted by the fashion, cosmetics, and media industries is physically unattainable for 99 percent of women. This is no accident, because if the ideal of beauty is physically unattainable, then consumers will never be satisfied, and therefore there will be an endless demand for beauty products."

This Jessica Johnston quote was taken from Viewpoint Three. Note how the author has taken care to quote Johnston exactly.

Paragraph 3

Abnormally thin women are used to sell more than just beauty products, however. They are also routinely used to sell products such as beer or cars that have—or should have—little to do with looks. One such advertisement for a brand of beer shows a dusty saloon filled with men. Suddenly, a scantily clad, exceedingly thin woman walks assertively into the bar and orders a drink. The bartender, paralyzed by her beauty, fumbles for the bottle opener. The woman rolls her eyes, clearly impatient. Without hesitating she grabs the beer from the bartender's hand, sticks it between her breasts, and snaps the cap off. A long shot of the bottle cap falling to the ground is an excuse to focus extendedly on the girl's slender midsection. All of the men in the bar gaze open-mouthed at the woman as she drinks her beer. These types of ads damage women's self-esteem and body image—and could cause them to hurt themselves chasing extreme thinness. According to Holly Hoff, program director of the National Eating Disorders Association, "The objectification of individuals based on their looks places a really unfortunate overemphasis on determining people's value and appeal based solely on their appearance. . . . We know when people set out to try [to] emulate these most often unhealthy and unattain-

The author describes the commercial using vivid and specific details to make it come alive for the reader.

The author quotes an authority who has extensive experience with eating disorders. Always make sure you quote authoritative sources in your essays.

able standards that they're seeing . . . they go to drastic eating and exercise behaviors that aren't necessarily healthy for them" (qtd. in Kirchheimer).

Paragraph 4

Nor are advertising's insidious messages limited to women. Men too are subjected to unrealistic standards that most would find incredibly difficult to meet. Consider the men usually featured in deodorant, aftershave, or other male-targeted commercials. Advertisements for Gillette's Mach 3 razor, for example, feature a shirtless, bronzed man with a muscled chest, bulging arms, and a perfect six-pack abdomen. Swathed in green light and set to turbo-charged music, this demigod flexes his muscles as he shaves his chisled chin clean. This image is supposed to reflect the average man undertaking his morning shave—but most men could not possibly attain this level of physical perfection.

Paragraph 5

This type of advertising negatively contributes to the low self-esteem and obsessive inadequacy that lead directly to eating disorders in both men and women. By cultivating an atmosphere where only the thinnest and most muscled fit in, advertisers drive American men and women toward harmful diets, extreme exercising, unhealthy weight loss products—even eating disorders. But companies have other options for selling their products. For example, in 2005 Dove Soap launched its successful "Campaign for Real Beauty" in which women, sizes 4–12, were photographed in their underwear. A stark contrast to the typical pouting, skeletal lingerie model, the Dove girls—none of whom were models—sent America a refreshing message: that real and healthy is real beautiful.

This is the essay's conclusion. Note how it returns to themes introduced earlier in the essay without repeating them verbatim.

The author ends her essay by offering suggestions for change or improvement.

Works Cited

Kirchheimer, Sid. "'Reality' TV Triggers Health Issues?" WebMD Medical News 28 Feb. 2003. < www.webmd. com/content/article/61/67538.htm > .

Johnston, Jessica. "Eating Disorders: Symptoms of a Sick Culture." Justice Nov. 2004–Jan. 2005.

Exercise A: Create an Outline from an Existing Essay

It often helps to create an outline of the five-paragraph essay before you write it. The outline can help you organize the information, arguments, and evidence you have gathered with your research.

For this exercise, create an outline that could have been used to write "Impossible Images: Advertising and Eating Disorders." This "reverse engineering" exercise is meant to help familiarize you with how outlines can help classify and arrange information.

To do this you will need to

1. articulate the essay's thesis
2. pinpoint important pieces of evidence
3. flag quotes that supported the essay's ideas, and
4. identify key points that supported the argument.

Part of the outline has already been started to give you an idea of the assignment.

Outline

Write the essay's thesis:

I. Introduction:

II. Paragraph 2
   A. Topic: Advertisers prey on women's insecurities to sell them beauty products
      i.

      ii. Jessica Johnston quote arguing that promoting unattainable body types fuels the demand for beauty products
III. Paragraph 3
   A. Topic: Unrealistic images of women in other types of advertising
      i.

ii. Holly Hoff quote about the danger of objectify-
   ing women

IV. Paragraph 4

   A. Topic:

     i.

     ii.

V. Write the essay's conclusion:

Thinspiration.com: The Deadly World of Online Eating Disorders

Editor's Notes The second model essay discusses a different aspect of eating disorders using the descriptive essay. This essay examines pro–eating disorder Web sites, a new and frightening online trend. The author argues that such Web sites should be shut down because they dangerously bait young women into developing eating disorders. She uses descriptive passages to make her ideas vivid and compelling and supports her points with facts and quotes.

As you read this essay, take note of its components and how they are organized (the sidebars in the margins provide further explanation).

Paragraph 1

Describe the way in which the author opens the essay. How does it differ from other essays? Does it grab your attention?

Before the Web site fully loads, a warning flashes across the screen: "Caution. This site contains pro–Eating Disorder images and information. If you do not have an eating disorder or are in recovery, do not enter this site." The curiosity of any reader is surely piqued. A click on the OK button prompts another warning: "Seriously. You enter this site of your own volition." But who could turn back now? Another OK button leads to a final warning: "So don't send me hate mail. It's not my fault if you don't like what you see." A final click is all it takes to slip into the eerily enchanting yet horrifying world of pro–eating disorder Web sites. Such Web sites dangerously package eating disorders as a lifestyle choice rather than the life-threatening disease that they are.

What is the essay's thesis statement?

Paragraph 2

What is the topic sentence of Paragraph 2?

One way in which such Web sites glorify eating disorders is by personifying the two most common ones, anorexia and bulimia, into goddess-like figures known to users as "Ana" and "Mia." Girls are encouraged to worship Ana and Mia (anorexics revere Ana, while bulimics reserve their devotion for Mia) as powerful deities that can grant their disturbing wish to waste away to nothing. Worship of the "goddesses" takes the form of bizarre rituals that might include praying, writing poetry or songs, or offering food to Ana or Mia. For example, a letter to Ana on one pro–eating disorder Web site offers the following glimpse into the worshipping mindset of one girl: "I offer you my soul, my heart and my bodily functions. . . . I seek your wisdom, your faith and your feather weight. I pledge to obtain the ability to float, to lower my weight to the single digits, I pledge to stare into space, to fear food, and to see obese images in the mirror. I will worship you and pledge to be a faithful servant until death does us part." Such sentiments alarmingly portray eating disorder sufferers like pilgrims on a noble spiritual quest.

What specific examples are used to illustrate the author's point?

Paragraph 3

Pro-Ana and pro-Mia sites also feature pictures of freakishly thin models, offered up to readers for "thinspiration." Most of these models appear scantily clad, their ribs and bones protruding from their gaunt, hollowed-out bodies. If they were not photographed wearing underwear and fashionable outfits, one might easily mistake them for prison camp inmates, wasting away behind cell walls. Further thinspiration comes from tips and tricks that essentially teach young women how to develop and then conceal their damaging disorder. For example, one site advises girls to take cold showers because it burns more calories. Another Web site suggests bulimics play a radio in the bathroom to cover sounds of purging after eating. It is reprehensible that the authors of these Web sites offer step-by-step instructions for how to give oneself an eating disorder. Becoming anorexic or bulimic is not a lifestyle one adopts, like becoming a vegetarian; it

What metaphors and similes are used throughout the essay?

What words does the author use to convey her opinion?

is a serious illness that men and women spend their lives trying to conquer—if death does not claim them first.

Paragraph 4

What is the topic sentence of Paragraph 4?

What adjectives are used in this essay? How does the author use them to paint a vivid picture?

Though they pretend to offer support to those suffering from eating disorders, in reality these Web sites encourage women to turn natural insecurities into a full-blown eating problem. Most women are insecure about some part of their body—it is normal to want to lose a bit of weight or to tone up muscle in some area. But the predatory world of online eating disorders encourages women to pick away at their flaws until they are unable to see any of their natural beauty at all. This was the experience of one teen author who stumbled upon pro-Ana Web sites. Though she felt sickened by the sites, she felt unable to look away from them. The more time she spent perusing the pro-Ana Web sites, "the more I began to criticize myself. I could see all of my own flaws: my flabby thighs, my chubby cheeks, everything was ugly. . . . I looked at myself in the mirror and started to cry. How could I feel good about myself when everything online told me I was too fat?" (*L.A. Youth* 11).

Paragraph 5

Why do you think the author chose this quote to support her point?

Pro-eating disorder Web sites are dangerous portals to a world that no girl should be baited into. Because recovery from eating disorders is such a painstaking and delicate process, the Web sites unfairly prey upon the insecurities of eating disorder victims, threatening to lure them back to the dangerous world they have worked so hard to leave behind. As Annie Hayashi, spokesperson for the National Association of Anorexia Nervosa and Associated Disorders (ANAD), says, "We believe that the pro–eating disorder sites are not only destructive but dangerous. . . . They give legitimacy to people who can't recover and are triggering for people who are trying to recover" (quoted in Depowski and Hart). Approximately 8 million Americans already suffer from anorexia, bulimia, and other eating disorders, as reported by ANAD. Should we allow pro–eating disorder Web sites to draw in more victims? For the safety of eating disorder sufferers and those who could become victims, pro–eating disorder Web sites should be shut down.

What is the essay's conclusion?

Works Cited

"How Thin Do I Have to Be?" <u>L.A. Youth</u>. Sept. 2005: 10–11.

Depowski, Kristin, and Kelly Hart. "'Pro-Ana' Websites Glorify Eating Disorders." <u>ABC News</u>. ABC. 13 June 2006. <www.abcnews.go.com/Health/story?id=Q0687 28&page=1>.

Exercise A: Create an Outline from an Existing Essay

As you did for the first model essay in this section, create an outline that could have been used to write "Thinspiration.com: The Deadly World of Online Eating Disorders." Be sure to identify the essay's thesis statement, its supporting ideas, its descriptive passages, and key pieces of evidence that were used.

Exercise B: Organize and Write Your Own Descriptive Five-Paragraph Essay

The second model essay includes descriptive passages that support a particular point of view about eating disorders. For this exercise, your assignment is to find supporting ideas, choose specific and concrete details, create an outline, and ultimately write a five-paragraph essay about any aspect of eating disorders you choose. Your goal is to use descriptive detail in an essay that either asserts an opinion about a topic (a persuasive essay) or explains the details of a topic (an expository essay).

Part 1: Write a Thesis Statement

Consider the following thesis statements for the focus of your essay:

- Pro–eating disorder Web sites should be shut down.
- Pro–eating disorder Web sites should not be shut down.
- There are a variety of different treatment options for those with eating disorders.
- It is impossible to recover fully from an eating disorder.

Or, see the sample paper topics suggested in Appendix D for more ideas.

Using information from some of the viewpoints in the previous section and from the information found in Section Three of this book, write down three arguments or pieces of evidence that support the thesis statement you selected. Then, for each of these three arguments, write down supportive facts, examples, and details that support it. These could be:

- Statistical information
- Personal memories and anecdotes
- Quotes from experts, peers, or family members
- Observations of people's actions and behaviors
- Specific and concrete details

The following topic sentence might be found in an essay on treatment options for eating disorders:

Example Paragraph Topic Sentence: In addition to psychiatric therapy and medical and nutritional programs, some alternative therapies have shown promise in helping patients control and conquer their eating disorders. Supporting pieces of evidence include:

- Healing gardens, as described in the text box accompanying Viewpoint One, can help patients learn to nurture themselves through the process of tending to plants.
- Art and dance therapy methods and other activities such as horseback riding and yoga have helped some patients find creative outlets for their emotions.
- Quote from Renfrew Center director Adrienne Ressler found in the text box that accompanies Viewpoint One: "Giving these women new interests and rituals replaces the negative rituals they have built around food."

Part 2: Place the information from Part I in outline form.

Part 3: Write the arguments or supporting statements in paragraph form.

You now have three arguments that support the paragraph's thesis statement, as well as supporting material. Use the outline to write out your three supporting arguments in paragraph form. Make sure each paragraph has a topic sentence that states the paragraph's thesis clearly and broadly. Then, add supporting sentences that express the facts, quotes, details, and examples that support the paragraph's argument. The paragraph may also have a concluding or summary sentence.

Part 4: Write an Introduction and Conclusion

Every essay features introductory and concluding paragraphs that are used to frame the main ideas being presented. Along with presenting the essay's thesis statement, well-written introductions should grab the attention of the reader and make clear why the topic being explored is important. The conclusion reiterates the essay's thesis and is also the last chance for the writer to make an impression on the reader. Strong introductions and conclusions can greatly enhance an essay's effect on an audience.

The Introduction

There are several techniques that can be used to craft an introductory paragraph. An essay can start with:

- an anecdote: a brief story that illustrates a point relevant to the topic;
- startling information: facts or statistics that elucidate the point of the essay;
- setting up and knocking down a position: a position or claim believed by proponents of one side of a controversy, followed by statements that challenge that claim;
- historical perspective: an example of the way things used to be that leads into a discussion of how or why things work differently now;
- summary information: general introductory information about the topic that feeds into the essay's thesis statement.

Problem One

Write an introduction for the essay you have outlined and partially written using one of the techniques described above.

The Conclusion

The conclusion brings the essay to a close by summarizing or returning to its main ideas. Good conclusions, however, go beyond simply repeating these ideas. Strong conclusions explore a topic's broader implications and reiterate why it is important to consider. They may frame the essay by returning to an anecdote featured in the opening paragraph. Or, they may close with a quotation or refer back to an event in the essay. In opinionated essays, the conclusion can reiterate which side the essay is taking or ask the reader to reconsider a previously held position on the subject.

Problem Two

Write a conclusion for the essay you have outlined and partially written using one of the techniques described above.

There Is No Perfect Body

Editor's Notes Essays drawn from memories or personal experiences are called personal narratives. The following essay is this type of essay. It is not based on research or the retelling of someone else's experiences, such as other descriptive essays you have read in this book. Instead this essay consists of an autobiographical story that recounts memories of an event that happened to someone who had an eating disorder. The essay differs from the first two model essays in that it is written in the subjective, or first-person ("I"), point of view. It is also different in that it is more than five paragraphs. Many ideas require more than five paragraphs in order to be adequately developed. Moreover, the ability to write a sustained paper is a valuable skill. Learning how to develop a longer piece of writing gives you the tools you will need to advance academically. Indeed, many colleges, universities, and academic programs require candidates to submit a personal narrative as part of the application process.

As you read the following essay, take note of the sidebars in the margin. Pay attention to how it is organized and presented.

Paragraph 1

The opening sentence establishes the essay's topic.

I never thought I would be the type to develop an eating disorder. I'm just your average, run-of-the-mill suburban teenager who comes from a nice town and a loving family. I've always liked food and for most of my life ate whatever I wanted without giving it a second thought. But seemingly out of nowhere I developed a dangerous eating disorder that nearly cost me my life—and put me on a long, arduous journey to recovery.

Paragraph 2

My obsession with my weight began around my junior year of high school. It was as if one day I woke up and could think of nothing else aside from that I felt incredibly *fat*. I felt as big as a house, weighed down like a water buffalo. I became convinced I was the fattest girl at my entire school. I became determined to lose weight. Over the next few months. I started cutting back on food, drastically reducing my calorie intake to sometimes as little as three hundred calories per day. I might eat a half a grapefruit in the morning, and then nothing besides gum, coffee, and diet soda for the rest of the day. I designated certain foods, such as lettuce or alfalfa sprouts, as "safe foods," meaning I could eat them and not feel badly about myself. I decided other foods were completely off-limits. Pasta, for example, became my worst enemy, though it had formerly been my favorite dish.

What metaphors and similes does the author use in this essay? What do they add to it?

Paragraph 3

Within three weeks I had dramatically changed the shape of my body, going from a size 10 to a size 2. I felt proud of myself, like all of my sacrificing and hard work had paid off. The trouble was, I still felt unsatisfied. Though I had expected to feel like everything in my life would fall into place once I became thin, I was disappointed to realize I felt more out of control than ever. Reaching my goal weight no longer mattered to me. In fact, I no longer had a specific goal, aside from being the thinnest girl anywhere I went. If I could just drop a few more pounds, I told myself, then all of my problems would disappear: I would be well liked, could focus on my school work, and feel great about myself.

Paragraph 4

After almost a year of nearly starving myself, my body began to undergo strange, frightening changes that I had not anticipated. My teeth took on a tinted yellow color that wouldn't come out, no matter how much I brushed. Worse, my hair became thin, dry, and brittle and began falling out in clumps. Other changes indicated something terrible was going on in my body: I stopped getting my

What transitions does the author use to keep sentences connected and moving forward?

period; my nails became hard and brittle; and ugly bruises began appearing randomly around my body, but I hadn't been hit or bumped into anything. I learned later that these are all signs of malnutrition. Finally, I began to notice a fine, feather-like hair growing all over my body. I later learned this is called lanugo, and it is the body's attempt to insulate itself in lieu of having fat.

Paragraph 5

What is the topic of Paragraph 5? How do you know this is the topic, even though there is no specific topic sentence?

I tried to hide this weird and scary hair growth by shaving all over my body—even my face, where it seemed to appear most prominently. I came up with other ways to hide the symptoms of my eating disorder from parents and friends, too. I started wearing big, baggy clothes to hide my bony frame, for example, and tried using extra conditioner in my hair to hide the thinning and limpness. I also religiously applied nail polish to mask my cracking, brittle fingernails.

Paragraph 6

What is the topic sentence of Paragraph 6?

But no matter what fixes I came up with, I couldn't hide my symptoms from my friends and family forever. One day, the lid was blown off my secret. I was feeling exceptionally dizzy that day—I hadn't eaten much in four days except for some tomatoes, an orange, and a few cans of diet soda—and my mother asked me to help her clean out the basement. As I lifted box after box, I felt myself growing weaker and weaker. I was so dizzy I started seeing spots. Suddenly there was a crash, and I realized I had fallen on the floor.

Paragraph 7

"Honey! Oh my God!" I heard my mother scream. "What's happened! Did you trip? Are you alright?!"

"Mom, I'm fine, I just need to. . . . " I tried to finish my sentence but couldn't even get the words out.

"Maybe you've overheated," my mom said. "I'm always saying that you shouldn't be wearing these baggy sweatshirts in eighty degree weather. Let me take that huge thing off of you."

As she reached for me, I panicked. I knew if she saw me—the real me—she would discover my terrible secret.

"Mom, no! Get off!" I yelled.

But I was too weak. My mother grabbed the hood of the oversized sweatshirt, which slipped easily off my tiny body. I heard her gasp in abject horror.

"Oh my God . . . what have you done to yourself?" She stared at me in disbelief. "Oh my baby . . . " She trailed off and began to cry.

Note how the dialogue between the narrator and her mother sounds natural and realistic. Can you picture the characters having this conversation?

Paragraph 8

That afternoon my parents took me to a doctor, who quickly diagnosed me with anorexia nervosa. In addition to telling my family that anorexia was a debilitating eating disorder that can be hidden for months, he told me I had done severe damage to my body, some of it possibly irreversible. He warned that if I continued starving myself, I would soon lose all of my hair and could lose the ability to have children someday. He also told me that I was at risk for having a fatal heart attack and for developing osteoporosis, a bone disorder that affects elderly women in which bones are weak, brittle, and easily broken.

What details about the physical effects of anorexia are included in this paragraph?

Paragraph 9

"Doctor, what do you recommend? I just don't know what to do," my mother sobbed. I quietly sat in the corner, embarrassed and ashamed that I had so severely threatened my health and caused my family so much grief.

"Your daughter is a very sick woman, I'm afraid," he said. He recommended that I be sent to a special facility, a hospital for eating disorder victims.

Paragraph 10

At first I was miserable at the hospital. The rooms and hallways had an unpleasant smell to them, like dried roses and rotten meat covered in bleach. I lost my privacy—I had

Is the author doing a good job of describing the hospital? What details help you envision it best?

to share a room with another girl named Maureen who was suffering from bulimia, an eating disorder in which she binged on food and then threw up to lose weight. Though at first I resented Maureen's constant presence, I soon began to see her—and the other girls at the hospital—as my friends and allies. After all, who else could better understand what I was going through than they?

Paragraph 11

Note how important the use of specific details is to imparting the author's experience.

Part of our treatment at the hospital was to follow a very strict schedule. Our days were so tightly managed I began to feel like a soldier in the army. We started each morning by being awoken at 5:30 A.M. and going to the nurse's station to be weighed and examined. We then were sent to a large dining hall for breakfast—they forced us to eat five meals a day, which was very difficult for me. I hated eating in public, and also eating every scrap of food on my plate. At home I used to discreetly spit food into a napkin or hide it up my sleeves to avoid eating it. At the hospital, though, nurses were watching to make sure I ate every bite. In between meals and snacks we met for individual and group therapy, which included sessions on coping skills and dealing with anger and sadness in healthy ways. We participated in other therapeutic activities such as yoga, horseback riding, and art. These activities helped me learn new ways to cope with the problems in my life, rather than attacking myself and restricting my food.

Paragraph 12

After three months in the facility, I was doing very well. I had learned to accept food as a healthy component of my life, and I eventually gained enough weight to be released from the facility. I was nervous about returning home: Would I be able to stick to my new, healthy lifestyle, or would I slip back into my old dangerous habits without the aid of the nurses to watch over me? I wish that I could say I was officially recovered from anorexia upon my release from the hospital, but recovery from eating disorders can be elusive. In fact, it is believed that only about 60 percent of people with severe eating disorders ever really recover. Would I be in that 60 percent? For my sake and my family's sake, I genuinely hope so. If I have learned one lesson from my experience, it is that we should all love ourselves, no matt_____ ___ _____ shape we come in—because there is no _____ _____ __dy.

How does this conclusion differ from nonpersonal essays? Note the differences. Do you find this conclusion effective?

Exercise A: Practice Writing a Scene with Dialogue

The previous model essay used scene and dialogue to make a point. For this exercise you will practice creative writing techniques to draft a one- or two-paragraph scene with dialogue. First, take another look at Essay Three and examine how dialogue is used.

When writing dialogue, it is important to:
1. use natural-sounding language;
2. include a few details showing characters' gestures and expressions as they speak;
3. avoid overuse of speaker tags with modifiers such as "he said stupidly," "she muttered softly," "I shouted angrily," and so on;
4. indent and create a new paragraph when speakers change;
5. place quotation marks at the beginning of and at the end of a character's speech. Do not enclose each sentence of a speech in quotation marks.

Scene Writing Practice

Interview a classmate, friend, or family member. Focus on a specific question that pertains to eating disorders, such as:

- What would you do if you knew someone with an eating disorder?
- What is your opinion of eating disorders?
- What do you think causes eating disorders?
- Have you ever felt like you had to lose weight? How did you handle doing so?
- Is there a difference between losing weight healthily and being diagnosed with an eating disorder? What are some of the differences?
- Have you ever worried that you were prone to eating disorders? Why?

Take notes while you interview your subject. Write down what he or she says as well as any details that are provided. Ask probing questions that reveal how the subject felt, what they said, and how they acted. Use your notes to create a brief one- or two-paragraph scene with dialogue.

But I Can't Write That

One aspect about personal narrative writing is that you are revealing to the reader something about yourself. Many people enjoy this part of writing. Others are not so sure about sharing their personal stories—especially if they reveal something embarrassing or something that could get them in trouble. In these cases, what are your options?

✔ Talk with your teacher about your concerns. Will this narrative be shared in class? Can the teacher pledge confidentiality?

✔ Change the story from being about yourself to a story about a friend. This will involve writing in the third person rather than the first person.

✔ Change a few identifying details and names to disguise characters and settings.

✔ Pick a different topic or thesis that you do not mind sharing.

Write Your Own Desciptive Five-Paragraph Essay

Using the information from this book, write your own five-paragraph descriptive essay that deals with eating disorders. You can use the resources in this book for information about eating disorders and how to structure a narrative essay.

The following steps are suggestions on how to get started.

Step One: Choose your topic.

The first step is to decide what topic to write your narrative essay on. Is there any subject that particularly fascinates you? Is there an issue you strongly support or feel strongly against? Is there a topic you feel personally connected to? Ask yourself such questions before selecting your essay topic. Refer to Appendix D: Sample Essay Topics on eating disorders if you need help selecting a topic.

Step Two: Write down questions and answers about the topic.

Before you begin writing, you will need to think carefully about what ideas your essay will contain. This is a process known as brainstorming. Brainstorming involves asking yourself questions and coming up with ideas to discuss in your essay. Possible questions that will help you with the brainstorming process include:

- Why is this topic important?
- Why should people be interested in this topic?
- How can I make this essay interesting to the reader?
- What question am I going to address in this paragraph or essay?
- What facts, ideas, or quotes can I use to support the answer to my question?

Questions especially for descriptive essays include:

- Have I chosen a compelling story to examine?
- Have I used vivid details?
- Have I made scenes come alive for my reader?

- What qualities do my characters have? Are they interesting?
- Does my descriptive essay have a clear beginning, middle, and end?
- Does my essay evoke a particular emotion or response from the reader?

Step Three: Gather facts, ideas, and anecdotes related to your topic.

This book contains several places to find information, including the viewpoints and the appendixes. In addition, you may want to research the books, articles, and Web sites listed in Section Three or do additional research in your local library. You can also conduct interviews if you know someone who has a compelling story that would fit well in your essay.

Step Four: Develop a workable thesis statement.

Use what you have written down in steps two and three to help you articulate the main point or argument you want to make in your essay. It should be expressed in a clear sentence and make an arguable or supportable point.

Example:

Although our media consistently features pictures of very thin women, such advertising has no bearing on whether American women develop eating disorders—otherwise, every single woman would develop one instead of less than 5 percent of women.

(This could be the thesis statement of a descriptive essay that argues against the claim that advertising and media cause eating disorders.)

Step Five: Write an outline or diagram.
1. Write the thesis statement at the top of the outline.
2. Write roman numerals I, II, and III on the left side of the page.
3. Next to each roman numeral, write down the best ideas you came up with in step three. These should all directly relate to and support the thesis statement.
4. Next to each letter, write down information that supports that particular idea.

Step Six: Write the three supporting paragraphs.
Use your outline to write the three supporting paragraphs. Write down the main idea of each paragraph in sentence form. Do the same thing for the supporting points of information. Each sentence should support the paragraph of the topic. Be sure you have relevant and interesting details, facts, and quotes. Use transitions when you move from idea to idea to keep the text fluid and smooth. Sometimes, although not always, paragraphs can include a concluding or summary sentence that restates the paragraph's argument.

Step Seven: Write the introduction and conclusion.
See Part 4 in Exercise B from Essay Two for information on writing introductions and conclusions.

Step Eight: Read and rewrite.
As you read, check your essay for the following:

✔ Does the essay maintain a consistent tone?

✔ Do all paragraphs reinforce your general thesis?

✔ Do all paragraphs flow from one to the other? Do you need to add transition words or phrases?

✔ Have you quoted from reliable, authoritative, and interesting sources?

✔ Is there a sense of progression throughout the essay?

✔ Does the essay get bogged down in too much detail or irrelevant material?

✔ Does your introduction grab the reader's attention?

✔ Does your conclusion reflect back on any previously discussed material or give the essay a sense of closure?

✔ Are there any spelling or grammatical errors?

Section Three: Supporting Research Material

Facts About Eating Disorders

Editor's Note: These facts can be used in reports or papers to reinforce or add credibility when making important points or claims.

Who Suffers from Eating Disorders?

According to the National Association of Anorexia Nervosa and Associated Disorders (ANAD), 7 million women and 1 million men suffer from eating disorders. Of these:

- 86 percent of eating disorder sufferers report onset of illness by the age of twenty.
- 43 percent onset between the ages of sixteen and twenty.
- 33 percent onset between the ages of eleven and fifteen.
- 10 percent report onset at ten years of age or younger.
- 77 percent report suffering from their eating disorders from one to fifteen years.
- 30 percent report duration from one to five years.
- 31 percent report duration from six to ten years.
- 16 percent report duration from eleven to fifteen years.
- An estimated 6 percent of serious cases die.
- Only 50 percent report being cured.

According to the Teen Health Centre based in Ontario:

- Eating disorders are the third most common chronic illness among adolescent females.
- One woman in one hundred will experience some form of eating disorder requiring medical attention within her lifetime. Among women aged fif-

teen to twenty-four years, the rate is one in fifteen women.
- 70 percent of normal weight adolescent girls feel fat and are engaged in negative eating behaviors to lose weight.
- Children as young as six years of age have developed negative attitudes about their body.

According to the National Institute of Mental Health:
- More than 90 percent of eating disorder sufferers are women.
- An estimated 0.5 to 3.7 percent of American women suffer from anorexia in their lifetime.
- An estimated 1.1 percent to 4.2 percent of American women have bulimia in their lifetime.
- An estimated 5 to 15 percent of people with anorexia or bulimia and an estimated 35 percent of those with binge-eating disorder are men.

Eating Disorder Fatality Statistics:
- Eating disorders have the highest mortality of any mental illness.
- 15 percent of people with anorexia die as a consequence of their condition.

Anorexia Is Characterized by the Following Behaviors:
- Deliberate self-starvation with weight loss
- Weighs 85 percent or less of what is considered normal for age and height
- Intense, persistent fear of gaining weight
- Refusal to eat or highly restrictive eating
- Continuous dieting
- Compulsive exercise
- Abnormal weight loss
- Sensitive to cold
- Absent or irregular menstruation
- Hair loss

Bulimia Is Characterized by the Following Behaviors:

- Preoccupation with food
- Binge eating, usually in secret
- Vomiting after bingeing
- Abuse of laxatives, diuretics, diet pills
- Denial of hunger or drugs to induce vomiting
- Compulsive exercise
- Swollen salivary glands
- Broken blood vessels in the eyes

The following physical symptoms may develop from anorexia:

- Menstrual periods cease
- Osteoporosis (thinning of the bones) through loss of calcium
- Hair and nails become brittle
- Skin dries and can take on a yellowish cast
- Mild anemia
- Muscles, including the heart muscle, waste away
- Severe constipation
- Drop in blood pressure, slowed breathing and pulse rates
- Internal body temperature falls, causing person to feel cold all the time
- Depression and lethargy

The following physical symptoms may develop from bulimia:

- Chronically inflamed and sore throat
- Swollen salivary glands in the neck and below the jaw
- Cheeks and face often become puffy, causing sufferers to develop a chipmunk-looking face
- Eroded tooth enamel, tooth decay from exposure to stomach acids
- Gastroesophageal reflux disorder from constant vomiting
- Intestinal problems from laxative abuse

- Kidney problems from abuse of diuretics (water pills)
- Severe dehydration from purging of fluids

Facts About Treatment for Eating Disorders

Treatment of anorexia calls for a specific program that involves three main phases: (1) restoring weight lost to severe dieting and purging; (2) treating psychological disturbances such as distortion of body image, low self-esteem, and interpersonal conflicts; and (3) achieving long-term remission and rehabilitation or full recovery.

According to ANAD:
- The treatment for anorexia and/or bulimia is often extremely expensive and can extend for several years.
- The cost of inpatient treatment can be thirty thousand dollars or more a month.
- The cost of outpatient treatment, including therapy and medical monitoring, can extend to one hundred thousand dollars or more.

Finding and Using Sources of Information

No matter what type of essay you are writing, it is necessary to find information to support your point of view. You can use sources such as books, magazine articles, newspaper articles, and online articles.

Using Books and Articles

You can find books and articles in a library by using the library's computer or cataloging system. If you are not sure how to use these resources, ask a librarian to help you. You can also use a computer to find many magazine articles and other articles written specifically for the Internet.

You are likely to find a lot more information than you can possibly use in your essay, so your first task is to narrow it down to what is likely to be most usable. Look at book and article titles. Look at book chapter titles and examine the book's index to see if it contains information on the specific topic you want to write about. (For example, if you want to write about bulimia and you find a book about eating disorders, check the chapter titles and index to be sure it contains information about bulimia before you bother to check out the book.)

For a five-paragraph essay, you do not need a great deal of supporting information, so quickly try to narrow down your materials to a few good books and magazine or Internet articles. You do not need dozens. You might even find that one or two good books or articles contain all the information you need.

You probably do not have time to read an entire book, so find the chapters or sections that relate to your topic and skim these. When you find useful information, copy it on a note card or in a notebook. You should look for supporting facts, statistics, quotations, and examples.

Using the Internet

When you select your supporting information, it is important that you evaluate its source. This is especially important with information you find on the Internet. Because nearly anyone can put information on the Internet, there is as much bad information as good information. Before using Internet information—or any information—try to determine if the source seems to be reliable. Is the author or Internet site sponsored by a legitimate organization? Is it from a government source? Does the author have any special knowledge or training relating to the topic you are looking up? Does the article give any indication of where its information comes from?

Using Your Supporting Information

When you use supporting information from a book, article, interview, or other source, there are three important things to remember:

1. Make it clear whether you are using a direct quotation or a paraphrase. If you copy information directly from your source, you are quoting it. You must put quotation marks around the information and tell where the information comes from. If you put the information in your own words, you are paraphrasing it.

   Here is an example of a using a quotation:

   Author Gracie Doran believes that Web sites that glorify anorexia and bulimia should be unequivocally shut down. Writes Doran, "Free speech is a good and necessary part of our society. However, one must think about the potential damage sites like these can cause to young girls and boys viewing this content. . . . People who support pro–eating disorder Web sites are wrongly justifying their disease and whether intentionally or not, are influencing people to join them."

Here is an example of a brief paraphrase of the same passage:

Gracie Doran is one person who believes that Web sites that glorify anorexia and bulimia should be unequivocally shut down. Such Web sites dangerously influence impressionable young girls and boys who may become prone to developing an eating disorder, she says. Though it is important to respect free speech and not unnecessarily censor material that some find unfavorable, pro-eating disorder Web sites do too much damage to justify keeping them operating.

2. Use the information fairly. Be careful to use supporting information in the way the author intended it. For example, it is unfair to quote an author as saying, "Anorexia is not a widespread problem" when he or she intended to say, "Anorexia is not a widespread problem among men over the age of 45." This is called taking information out of context. This is using supporting evidence unfairly.

3. Give credit where credit is due. Giving credit is known as citing. You must use citations when you use someone else's information, but not every piece of supporting information needs a citation.
   - If the supporting information is general knowledge—that is, it can be found in many sources—you do not have to cite your source.
   - If you directly quote a source, you must cite it.
   - If you paraphrase information from a specific source, you must cite it.

If you do not use citations where you should, you are *plagiarizing*—or stealing—someone else's work.

Citing Your Sources

There are a number of ways to cite your sources. Your teacher will probably want you to do it in one of three ways:

- Informal: As in the example above, you tell where you got the information in the same place you use it.
- Informal list: At the end of the article, place an unnumbered list called Works Consulted of the sources you used. This tells the reader where, in general, you got your information.
- Formal: Use a Works Cited list. A Works Cited list is generally placed at the end of an article or essay, although it may be located in different places depending on your teacher's requirements.

Works Cited

Doran, Gracie. "Everything Online Should Not Be Digested." <u>Daily Evergreen</u> 13 July 2006. < www.dailyevergreen.com/ story/18243 > .

Using MLA Style to Create a Works Cited List

You will probably need to create a list of works cited in your paper. A Works Cited list includes materials that you quoted from, paraphrased, or summarized. When you also include other works you consulted in your research, call this section Works Consulted. There are several different ways to structure these references. The following examples are based on Modern Language Association (MLA) style, one of the major citation styles used by writers.

Book Entries

For most book entries you will need the author's name, the book's title, where it was published, what company published it, and the year it was published. This information is usually found on the inside of the book. Variations on book entries include the following:

A book by a single author:
Guest, Emma. <u>Children of AIDS: Africa's Orphan Crisis.</u> London: Sterling, 2003.

Two or more books by the same author:
Friedman, Thomas L. *From Beirut to Jerusalem.* New York: Doubleday, 1989.
---. <u>The World Is Flat: A Brief History of the Twentieth Century.</u> New York: Farrar, 2005.

A book by two or more authors:
Pojman, Louis P., and Jeffrey Reiman. <u>The Death Penalty: For and Against.</u> Lanham: Rowman, 1998.

A book with an editor:
Friedman, Lauri S., ed. <u>At Issue: What Motivates Suicide Bombers?</u> San Diego: Greenhaven, 2004.

Periodical and Newspaper Entries

Entries for sources found in periodicals and newspapers are cited a bit differently from books. For one, these sources usually have a title and a publication name. They also may have specific dates and page numbers. Unlike book entries, you do not need to list where newspapers or periodicals are published or what company publishes them.

An article from a periodical:
> Snow, Keith Harmon. "State Terror in Ethiopia." <u>Z Magazine</u> June 2004: 33–35.

An article from a newspaper:
> Constantino, Rebecca. "Fostering Love, Respecting Race." <u>Los Angeles Times</u> 14 Dec. 2002: B17.

Internet Sources

To document a source you found online, try to provide as much information on it as possible, including the author's name, the title of the document, date of publication or of last revision, your date of access, and the URL (enclosed in angle brackets).

A Web source:
> Shyovitz, David. "The History and Development of Yiddish." <u>Jewish Virtual Library.</u> 30 May 2005 < www.jewishvirtuallibrary.org/jsource/ History/yiddish.html > .

Your teacher will tell you exactly how information should be cited in your essay. Generally, the very least information needed is the original author's name, the name of the article or other publication, and the URL of the page you are citing.

Be sure you know exactly what information your teacher requires before you start looking for your supporting information so that you know what information to record in your notes.

Sample Essay Topics

Eating Disorders Are a Disease
Eating Disorders Are Not a Disease
Eating Disorders Are a Growing Problem
The Prevalence of Eating Disorders Is Exaggerated
Eating Disorders in America
Eating Disorders Around the World
Defining Different Types of Eating Disorders
Eating Disorders and White Women
Eating Disorders and Women of Color
Males Are at Risk for Eating Disorders
Athletes Are at Risk for Eating Disorders
Pre-teens Are at Risk for Eating Disorders
Adults Are at Risk for Eating Disorders
The Media Encourages People to Develop Eating
  Disorders
The Media Has No Bearing on Whether People
  Develop Eating Disorders
America Is Obsessed with Thinness
America Is Not Obsessed with Thinness
Psychological Factors Cause Eating Disorders
Low Self-Esteem Causes Eating Disorders
Peer Pressure Causes Eating Disorders
Biological Factors Cause Eating Disorders
Environmental Factors Cause Eating Disorders
Recovery from Eating Disorders Is Possible
Recovery from Eating Disorders Is Not Possible
Treatment Options for Eating Disorders
Parents Can Help Prevent Eating Disorders
The Government Can Help Prevent Eating Disorders
Schools Can Help Prevent Eating Disorders
Pro–Eating Disorder Web Sites Should Be Shut Down
Pro–Eating Disorder Web Sites Should Not Be Shut
  Down

Organizations to Contact

American Anorexia/Bulimia Association of Philadelphia (AA/BA)
4200 Monument Ave., Philadelphia, PA 19131 • (215) 877-2000 • e-mail: jbsmje@epix.net • Web site: www. aabaphila.org

AA/BA is a nonprofit organization that works to prevent eating disorders by informing the public about their prevalence, early warning signs, and symptoms. AA/BA also provides information about effective treatments to sufferers and their families and friends.

American Psychiatric Association (APA)
1000 Wilson Blvd., Suite 1825, Arlington, VA 22209-3901 (703) 907-7300 • e-mail: apa@psych.org • Web site: www. psych.org

APA is an organization of psychiatrists dedicated to studying the nature, treatment, and prevention of mental disorders, including those that contribute to eating disorders. It helps create mental health policies, distributes information about psychiatry, and promotes psychiatric research and education.

American Psychological Association (APA)
750 First St. NE, Washington, DC 20002-4242 • (202) 336-5500 • (800) 374-2721 • e-mail: public.affairs@apa.org Web site: www.apa.org

A scientific and professional organization that represents psychology in the United States. With 150,000 members, the APA is the largest association of psychologists worldwide. It produces numerous publications on eating disorders and other topics related to psychology.

Anorexia Nervosa and Related Eating Disorders, Inc. (ANRED)

PO Box 5102, Eugene, OR 97405 • (503) 344-1144 • Web site: www.anred.com

ANRED is a nonprofit organization that provides information about anorexia nervosa, bulimia nervosa, binge-eating disorder, compulsive exercising, and other lesser-known food and weight disorders, including details about recovery and prevention. ANRED offers workshops, individual and professional training, as well as local community education. It also produces a monthly newsletter.

Eating Disorders Awareness and Prevention, Inc. (EDAP)

603 Stewart St., Suite 803, Seattle, WA 98101 • (206) 382-3587 • toll-free information and referral helpline: (800) 931-2237 • email: info@NationalEatingDisorders.org • Web site: www.edap.org

EDAP is dedicated to promoting the awareness and prevention of eating disorders by encouraging positive self-esteem and size acceptance. It provides free and low-cost educational information on eating disorders and their prevention. EDAP also provides educational outreach programs and training for schools and universities and sponsors the Puppet Project for Schools and the annual National Eating Disorders Awareness Week. EDAP publishes a prevention curriculum for grades four through six as well as public prevention and awareness information packets, videos, guides, and other materials.

Harvard Eating Disorders Center (HEDC)

356 Boylston St., Boston, MA 02118 • (888) 236-1188 • Web site: www.hedc.org

HEDC is a national nonprofit organization dedicated to advancing the field of eating disorders through research, training, education, and outreach. It works to expand knowledge about eating disorders and their detection, treatment, and prevention and promotes the healthy development of women, children, and everyone at risk. A primary goal for the organization is lobbying for health policy initiatives on behalf of individuals with eating disorders.

National Association of Anorexia and Associated Disorders (ANAD)

PO Box 7, Highland Park, IL 60035 • (847) 831-3438 • Web site: www.anad.org

ANAD offers hotline counseling, operates an international network of support groups for people with eating disorders and their families, and provides referrals to health-care professionals who treat eating disorders. It produces a quarterly newsletter and information packets and organizes national conferences and local programs. All ANAD services are provided free of charge.

National Eating Disorder Information Centre (NEDIC)

ES 7-421, 200 Elizabeth Street, Toronto, ON M5G 2C4, CANADA • 1-866-NEDIC-20 (1-866-633-4220) • e-mail: nedic@uhn.on.ca • Web site: www.nedic.ca/index.shtml

NEDIC is a Toronto-based organization that provides information and resources on eating disorders and weight preoccupation. It focuses on the sociocultural factors that influence female health-related behaviors. NEDIC promotes healthy lifestyles and encourages individuals to make informed choices based on accurate information. It publishes a newsletter and a guide for families and friends of eating disorder sufferers and sponsors Eating Disorders Awareness Week in Canada.

Society for Adolescent Medicine (SAM)

1916 NW Copper Oaks Cir., Blue Springs, MO 64015 • (816) 224-8010 • Web site: www.adolescenthealth.org

SAM is a multidisciplinary organization of professionals committed to improving the physical and psychosocial health and well-being of all adolescents. It helps plan and coordinate national and international professional education programs on adolescent health. Its publications include the monthly *Journal of Adolescent Health* and the quarterly *SAM Newsletter.*

Bibliography

Books

Arnold Anderson, *Making Weight: Healing Men's Conflicts with Food, Weight, and Shape.* San Diego: Gurze, 2000.

Katie S. Bagley, *Eat Right: Tips for Good Nutrition.* Mankato, MN: Capstone, 2001.

Marjolijn K. Bijlefeld and Sharon Zoumbaris, *Food and You: A Guide to Healthy Habits for Teens.* Westport, CT: Greenwood, 2001.

Hilde Bruch, *The Golden Cage: The Enigma of Anorexia Nervosa.* Cambridge, MA: Harvard University Press, 2001.

Joan Jacobs Brumberg, *Fasting Girls: The History of Anorexia Nervosa.* New York: Vintage, 2000.

Julie M. Clarke and Ann Kirby-Payne, *Understanding Weight and Depression.* New York: Rosen, 2000.

Lawrence Clayton, *Diet Pill Drug Dangers.* Springfield, NJ: Enslow, 2001.

Julia K. De Pree, *Body Story.* Athens: Swallow Press/Ohio University Press, 2004.

Eve Eliot, *Insatiable—The Compelling Story of Four Teens, Food, and Its Power.* Deerfield Beach, FL: Life Issues, 2001.

Kathlyn Gay, *Eating Disorders: Anorexia, Bulimia, and Binge Eating.* Berkeley Heights, NJ: Enslow, 2003.

Tracey Gold, *Room to Grow: An Appetite for Life.* Beverly Hills: New Millennium, 2003.

Lori Gottlieb, *Stick Figure: A Diary of My Former Self.* New York: Berkley, 2001.

Jennifer Hendricks, *Slim to None: A Journey Through the Wasteland of Anorexia Treatment.* Chicago: Contemporary, 2003.

Marlys C. Johnson, *Understanding Exercise Addiction.* New York: Rosen, 2000.

Jim Kirkpatrick and Paul Caldwell, *Eating Disorders: Anorexia Nervosa, Bulimia, Binge Eating and Others*. Buffalo, NY: Firefly, 2001.

Caroline Knapp, *Appetites: Why Women Want*. New York: Counterpoint, 2003.

Alexander R. Lucas, *Demystifying Anorexia Nervosa: An Optimistic Guide to Understanding and Healing*. New York: Oxford University Press, 2004.

Morgan Menzie, *Diary of an Anorexic Girl*. Nashville: W, 2003.

Lisa Messinger and Merle Cantor Goldberg, *My Thin Excuse: Understanding, Recognizing, and Overcoming Eating Disorders*. Garden City Park, NY: Square One, 2006.

Deborah Marcontell Michel, *When Dieting Becomes Dangerous: A Guide to Understanding and Treating Anorexia and Bulimia*. New Haven, CT: Yale University Press, 2003.

Heather Moehn, *Understanding Eating Disorder Support Groups*. New York: Rosen, 2000.

Mimi Nichter, *Fat Talk: What Girls and Their Parents Say About Dieting*. Cambridge, MA: Harvard University Press, 2000.

Christie Pettit, *Starving: A Personal Journey Through Anorexia*. Grand Rapids, MI: F.H. Revell, 2003.

Linda M. Rio and Tara M. Rio, *The Anorexia Diaries: A Mother and Daughter's Triumph over Teenage Eating Disorders*. Emmaus, PA: Rodale, 2003.

Ira M. Sacker, *Dying to Be Thin: Understanding and Defeating Anorexia Nervosa and Bulimia*. New York: Warner, 2001.

Pamela M. Smith, *The Diet Trap*. Washington, DC: Regnery, 2000.

Debbie Stanley, *Understanding Sports and Eating Disorders*. New York: Rosen, 2000.

Michael A. Strober and Meg F. Schneider, *Just a Little Too Thin: How to Pull Your Child Back from the Brink of an Eating Disorder*. Cambridge, MA: Da Capo, 2006.

C.L. Watson, *Eating the Shadow: A Memoir of Loss and Recovery*. Stone Ridge, NY: Fenn, 2006.

Jonathan Watson, *Male Bodies: Health, Culture, and Identity*. London: Taylor and Francis, 2000.

Periodicals

Janet Bailey, "Eating Disorders: Are You at Risk?" *Redbook*, October 2002.

Katarzyna Bisaga, et al., "Eating Disorder and Depressive Symptoms in Urban High School Girls from Different Ethnic Backgrounds," *Journal of Developmental and Behavioral Pediatrics*, August 2005.

Black Issues in Higher Education, "Anorexia, Bulimia Becoming 'Equal Opportunity Disorders,'" April 21, 2005.

Kristin Cobb, "His-and-Her Hunger Pangs," *Science News*, July 6, 2002.

Barbara Curtis, "When Dieting Spells Danger," *Christian Parenting Today*, Summer 2002.

Karen Dias, "The Ana Sanctuary: Women's Pro-Anorexia Narratives in Cyberspace," *Journal of International Women's Studies*, April 2003.

Deirdre Dolan, "Learning to Love Anorexia? Pro-Ana Web Sites Flourish," *New York Observer*, July 29, 2004.

Galina Espinoza, "Diary of a Food Fight," *People*, March 31, 2003.

Harvard Mental Health Letter, "Anorexia Nervosa, Part II," March 2003.

Bruce Jancin, "Anxiety Disorders, Depression Found in Former Anorexics," *Clinical Psychiatry News*, August 2003.

Allan S. Kaplan, "Compulsory Refeeding in Anorexia: Beneficial or Harmful?" *Journal of Addiction and Mental Health*, May–June 2002.

Kathiann M. Kowalski, "Body Image: How Do You See Yourself?" *Current Health 2*, March 2003.

Dawn Mackeen, "Waifs on the Web," *Teen People*, April 1, 2002.

Richard Morgan, "The Men in the Mirror," *Chronicle of Higher Education*, September 27, 2002.

Peggy O'Farrell, "Anorexia Increasing, Treatment Shrinking: Families Struggle Against Eating Disorder," *Cincinnati Enquirer*, September 5, 2002.

Terry O'Neill, "Death Wish I: Dying to be Skeletal," *Report Newsmagazine*, January 21, 2002.

Jessica Reaves, "Anorexia Goes High Tech," *Time*, July 31, 2001.

Susan Schindehette, "Recipe for Life: A Breakthrough Therapy Brings Hope to Young Girls—and the Families—Who Suffer from Anorexia," *People*, December 15, 2003.

Ellen M. Shaw, "The Dangers of Eating Disorders," *American Fitness*, January–February 2002.

Mim Udovitch, "A Secret Society of the Starving," *New York Times Magazine*, September 8, 2002.

Internet Source

Kyffin Webb, "Anorexia: From Control to Chaos," Alternet, February 5, 2002. www.alternet.org.

Web Sites

Eating Disorder Referral and Information Center (www.edreferral.com). Provides information and treatment resources for all types of eating disorders. Offers eating disorder victims help finding medical professionals.

Eating Disorders Association (EDA) (www.edauk.com). A British Web site containing information on aspects of eating disorders including anorexia nervosa, bulimia nervosa, binge-eating disorder, and related eating disorders.

Something Fishy Website on Eating Disorders (www. something-fishy.com). An extensive Web site dedicated to raising awareness about eating disorders and providing information about recovery. Contains information about treatment, articles, first-person narratives, and more. An excellent resource.

Index

Picture Credits

About the Editor

Lauri S. Friedman earned her bachelor's degree in religion and political science from Vassar College. Her studies there focused primarily on political Islam, and she produced a thesis on the Islamic Revolution in Iran titled *Neither West, Nor East, But Islam*. She also holds a preparatory degree in flute performance from the Manhattan School of Music. The numerous publications she has edited for Greenhaven Press have focused on controversial social issues such as gay marriage, Islam, terrorism, and the Patriot Act. She has also authored several young adult publications, including titles on the death penalty and a biography of Michael Dell for Reference Point Press and Morgan Reynolds Publishing. Lauri is currently the head of undergraduate admissions at the University of California, San Diego. She lives near the beach in San Diego with her partner, Randy, and their yellow lab, Trucker.

Eating disorders